Book
of
Babies

Tradition, Trivia & Curious Facts

Lisa Wojna
Illustrations by Peter Tyler and Roger Garcia

BLUE
BIKE
BOOKS

Book *of* Babies

Tradition, Trivia & Curious Facts

© 2008 by Blue Bike Books
First printed in 2008 10 9 8 7 6 5 4 3 2 1
Printed in Canada

The Publisher: Blue Bike Books
Website: www.bluebikebooks.com

Library and Archives Canada Cataloguing in Publication

Wojna, Lisa, 1962–
  Book of babies : tradition, trivia & curious facts / by Lisa Wojna.

Includes bibliographical references.

ISBN 978-1-897278-53-6

  1. Infants—Miscellanea. 2. Toddlers—Miscellanea. I. Title.

HQ774.W63 2009   305.232   C2008-906466-6

Project Director: Nicholle Carrière
Project Editor: Kathy van Denderen
Cover Image: Courtesy of Dreamstime; © Dolgachov I Dreamstime.com
Illustrations: Peter Tyler and Roger Garcia

We acknowledge the support of the Alberta Foundation for the Arts for our publishing program.

We acknowledge the financial support of the Government of Canada through
the Book Publishing Industry Development Program (BPIDP) for our publishing
activities.

 Canadian   Patrimoine
Heritage   canadien

PC: 1

DEDICATION

To my grandson Seth. The latest precious baby in my life.

CONTENTS

ACKNOWLEDGMENTS

As always, this project wouldn't be possible without the ongoing support of my family—Garry, Peter, Melissa, Matthew, Nathan and Jada. I love you all!

Any writer will attest to the fact that a great book is really a partnership—a writer needs a great editor. This project drew the best card when it came to landing an editor. Thank you so much, Kathy, for your eagle eye, your methodical mind and that fine-toothed comb you use to pick out all the snags in your projects. You're precious…really. And I love you dearly!

To Nicholle and Blue Bike Books, who believed in this project in the first place. And to Faye—dear friend and mentor, even though I'm always giving you a hard time.

INTRODUCTION

Twenty-seven years ago, as of the writing of this book, I discovered I was pregnant with my first child. My husband, on learning the news, came home from work that day with a single red rose, Dr. Spock's book *Childbirth Without Fear* and a pipe. The flower was sweet. The book made me tremble—up to that point I didn't know I should be scared! The pipe, my husband's new vice, I battled for the next 18 years. But the baby was a dream whom every week, every month, every trimester milestone I came to love more and more. And when he finally arrived, he was perfect in every way—his siblings eventually nicknamed him the "Golden Child."

There were three more "tummy children," as I call them: Melissa, my only little girl for almost 20 years; Matthew, the little boy I called "my only sunshine"; Nathan, my sick little baby who fought back from heart surgery. And then, in 2005, I witnessed the birth of my first grandchild—baby Jada. From the time she was four months old, she was living with us full time. Shortly thereafter we adopted her, and she became my "heart baby." I am now the mother of five children, and in February 2008, I was on hand to welcome to the world our family's latest addition—my grandson Seth. To say these children are my life is an understatement—you never know how much you can love someone until a baby comes along.

Being a mother, and now a grandmother, and being a writer are the most important things in my life. So when I began to write this book, I couldn't think of a better way of binding these loves. And every step of the way has been a learning experience. I was amazed at how much I didn't know about the development of the fetus. I laughed my way through my research on celebrity baby names. And I marveled at the stories of love and courage with which many families cope with challenging situations.

It must be said, however, that this book is not a primer for the newly pregnant. It's not a how-to manual. It is not a medical textbook. I do not claim to be a parenting guru overflowing with concrete information that will dispel all your fears and replace the need to hire a super nanny. In fact, many of the claims to fame included in this book—such as the oldest woman to give birth—are being challenged every day.

What this book does promise is a lot of laughs, a fun way for anyone—parent, grandparent, aunt or uncle or just you and your really good friends—to pass an afternoon learning everything you ever wanted to know about babies. And if you or someone you know is expecting, and you're planning a baby shower, this book will be a great resource for an afternoon of trivia games. I guarantee you'll run out of time before you run out of questions!

So relax, kick off your shoes and sit back with a nice cup of tea and enjoy. After all, who can resist a baby? After reading this book, you'll love babies even more!

MARKING THE MIRACLES

Since the dawn of time folks have been joining together for the sole purpose of creating babies—or at least that was one official reason behind the intimacy that accompanies marriage. In this action of mating and making offspring, we're no different from our friends in the animal kingdom. We're simply ensuring the continuation of our species.

However, sometime during the development of the human race it became apparent that this birthing thing was quite a challenge. Mothers and babies died during this very "natural" process. Something had to be done. Various cultures and communities began developing birthing procedures that helped both mom and babe. Midwives or doulas took on the responsibility of helping women deliver their newborns. The evolution of medical science produced

*doctors who specialized in obstetrics. And statisticians got
busy keeping track of things such as the age of women giving
birth and the trends towards low birth weights or the use of
cesarean sections—all this helps in the development of better
and safer methods to assist women to give birth. What
follows is just a sampling of what those numbers look like.*

Welcome to the World!

According to the Central Intelligence Agency (CIA) in the
United States, more than a quarter of the world's population is
under the age of 15. That could be because every year we welcome an estimated 160 million births.

Questionable Statistics

Because something like determining the number of babies born
around the world every day, let alone every minute, isn't a simple
task, several numbers are bandied about by different sources.
One suggests that a baby is born every three seconds. Another
more temperate estimate is that one baby is born every eight seconds. While that seems like a lot, and you might be wondering
how our old Mother Earth can handle such a population explo-
sion, people are regularly dying too. One web source states that
"one person every other second needlessly dies"—at the time of
this writing that was an estimated 7,663,015 people—from
"starvation, waterborne diseases and AIDS." And that's not
including the people around the world dying from illness, acci-
dents and other tragedies.

On the other hand, the CIA reported in its *World Factbook* that
in July 2008 the world's population was estimated at
6,706,993,152. How many babies make up that statistic you ask?

Their figures cite an overall population growth of 1.188 percent, or an average of 20.18 births per 1000 population. Worldwide, the infant mortality rate is an estimated 42.09 deaths per 1000 live births. If you average out all the babies born in the world and all the women of birthing age, every woman could have 2.61 children.

Countries with the Highest Birth Rate
Depending on the source, there are a few interpretations on the 10 countries with the highest birth rates. The listing below is based on 2006 crude birth rate estimates from the United Nations Population Division:

Rank	Country	Birth Rate (per 1000 persons)
1.	Democratic Republic of Congo	49.6
2.	Guinea-Bissau	49.6
3.	Liberia	49.6
4.	Niger	49.0
5.	Afghanistan	48.2
6.	Mali	48.1
7.	Angola	47.3
8.	Burundi	47.1
9.	Uganda	46.6
10.	Sierra Leone	46.2

Countries with the Lowest Birth Rate

Depending on the source, there are also a few interpretations of the 10 countries with the lowest birth rates. The listing below is based on 2006 crude birth rate estimates from the United Nations Population Division, which only lists statistics for 195 countries:

Rank	Country	Birth Rate (per 1000 persons)
1.	Hong Kong	7.6
2.	Macau	7.6
3.	Germany	8.2
4.	Singapore	8.2
5.	Japan	8.3
6.	Bosnia and Herzegovina	8.8
7.	Bulgaria	8.9
8.	Croatia	9.0
9.	Slovenia	9.0
10.	Lithuania	9.1

Where Are You, Canada?

In case you were wondering, the United Nations Population Division places Canada way down the list when it comes to birth rate per population comparisons. It sits at the 169th spot in the 195 countries tallied.

Canadian Trends

Canada's burgeoning population, according to Stats Canada figures for 2005:

☛ There were 342,176 live births.

☛ Men outnumbered the women, with 175,376 of newborns being male and the remaining 166,800 female.

☛ Of the total number of babies born, 356 weighed less than 500 grams (17.6369 ounces).

☛ On the heavier end of the scale, 66 babies were born at 5500 grams (12.2 pounds) and heavier.

☛ From a geographic standpoint, the province with the largest number of babies born was Ontario, with 133,760 recorded live births. Of course, that only makes sense because, with 12,753,702 people, it's the Canadian province with the largest population.

☛ Quebec saw the second highest number of babies born, with 76,346 live births.

☛ Alberta was in third place, with 42,110 live births.

☛ Although almost a million more people live in British Columbia than Alberta, BC's birth rate in 2005 was slightly smaller, with 40,827.

☛ 14,145 live births were recorded in Manitoba.

☛ Saskatchewan saw its population grow with the birth of 11,967 babies.

☛ Nova Scotians welcomed 8557 newborns.

☛ New Brunswick wasn't far behind that with 6892 live births that same year.

☛ Newfoundland and Labrador said hello to 4501 bundles of joy.

☛ 1340 babes were born in Prince Edward Island.

☞ The Northwest Territories recorded 712 live births.

☞ 699 babies were born in Nunavut.

☞ 320 newborns saw the light of day in the Yukon.

U.S. Baby Stats

The following was compiled using information from the Centers for Disease Control and Prevention National Center for Health Statistics.

☞ In 2006, a total of 4,265,555 babies were born in the United States.

☞ Of the babies born that year, 3,310,308 were white, 666,481 were black, 241,045 were Asian or Pacific Islander and 47,721 were Native American.

☞ The largest number of babies, 1,181,899 of them, were born to mothers in the 25–29 age bracket. A close second were mothers aged 20–24, birthing 1,080,437 babies.

☞ The 2006 stats suggest older women are also choosing to become mothers in fairly substantial numbers. Women in the 40–44 age bracket welcomed 105,539 babies; another 6480 babies were born to women in the 45–49 age bracket; and women aged 50–54 birthed 494 babies.

☞ The greatest number of babies in 2006, 2,303,019 of them, were born between 37 and 39 weeks gestation.

☞ 1,656,342 babies weighed between 6 pounds, 10 ounces, and 7 pounds, 12 ounces.

☞ A staggering 4550 babies born in 2006 weighed between 11 and 18 pounds.

☞ In 2006, there were 2,929,590 vaginal deliveries and 1,321,054 C-sections. Another 14,911 deliveries are unstated.

The following information was retrieved from the U.S. Census Bureau.

- In 1970 the average age for a woman in the United States to give birth for the first time was 21.4 years. In 2002, that average age increased to 25.1 years.

- In 1976, 36 percent of mothers had four or more children. In 2002, that number dropped to 10 percent.

- In 1989 a staggering 42 percent of pregnant women smoked. That number has dropped significantly, but in 2002 there were still 11.4 percent of pregnant women who reported smoking.

- In 2001 there were an estimated 69,000 daycares in the U.S.

- The preference for the use of midwives has increased since 1975, when less than one percent of women reported using one. In 2002, that number increased to 8.1 percent.

- The hospital was the place of delivery for 99 percent of all live births in 2002. A total of 35,416 births took place somewhere other than a traditional hospital setting: 22,980 births were at home; 9683 were at a freestanding birthing center; 385 were in a clinic or doctor's office; 2368 were listed as "other" and 120 weren't specified.

- In 1990, 75 percent of pregnant women received pre-natal care. That number increased to 84 percent in 2003.

- In 2004 there were an estimated 82.5 million mothers in the country.

- Mississippi took the top spot when it came to recording the country's highest teen birth rate in 2006, with 60 of 1000 births to teenaged moms.

- In 2006, the American state with the lowest teen birth rate was New Hampshire, with 19 of 1000 live births born to teen moms.

☛ The largest number of babies born in a single year in the United States occurred in 1961, with 4,268,326 births recorded.

DID YOU KNOW?

According to the American Dietetic Association, the average pregnant woman should consume somewhere between 2500 and 2700 calories per day. That's about 300 calories per day more than usual.

Average Birth Weights

☛ Between 2004 and 2006, the average birth weight of babies born in the Netherlands was 3434 grams (7.57 pounds).

☛ In 2007, the Canadian Institute for Health Information reported that one in 16 births were listed as low birth weight babies. According to the World Health Organization (WHO), babies born less than 2500 grams (5.5 pounds) are considered low birth weight babies.

☛ According to statistics collected between 1995 and 1997, a pregnant woman in the United States can expect to deliver a full-term baby weighing anywhere between 6 pounds and 9 pounds, 4 ounces. If you average out all the figures, the median birth weight in the U.S. is around 7 pounds, 11 ounces.

DID YOU KNOW?

According to diehard number crunchers at the Population Reference Bureau in Washington, DC, you, yes, you reading this book, are one of the 106,000,000,000 people who have been born throughout the history of this world we call home.

THE STATISTICS

In back rooms across countries around the world, there are volumes of number crunchers, as well as multiple volumes of their work, outlining what the social fabric of our world looks like. Of course, numbers often change, depending on the source recording the information, the questions asked and the people asking them, but the results do serve to give us an idea of what folks are generally up to.

Canadian Mothers and Birth Rates

Here's what Stats Canada has to say in regard to births in 2004:

☞ The crude birth rate is defined as the "number of live births for every 1000 people in the population." In 2008, Canada's birth rate is estimated at 10.29. Compare this to 2004, when the birth rate was 10.5, which demonstrates a slow but steady decline over the years.

☞ Nova Scotia, Quebec, Ontario, Alberta and the Yukon were the only regions in Canada that recorded an increase in the number of babies born.

☞ Births declined by three percent in Newfoundland and Labrador.

☞ Women in Newfoundland and Labrador had almost exactly 50 percent fewer babies than they did in 1983 (8929 in 1983, and 4488 in 2004).

☞ If statistics are any indication, Canadian mothers are getting older. On average, new mothers in 2004 were 29.7 years old.

☞ In 2004, 20.6 percent of mothers were 24 years of age or younger. Twenty-five years earlier, 40.7 percent of all mothers were in that age group.

☞ Most Canadian mothers (62.1 percent) were between 25 and 34 years of age.

☞ Canadian women are choosing to have children later in life: 17.2 percent of new mothers were 35 years or older, whereas in 1979, the percentage of new mothers in that age group was only 4.6 percent.

☞ "Fertility rate" is defined as "an estimate of the average number of children that women will have during the years they are aged 15 to 49." In 2004, Canada's fertility rate was

1.53 children per woman. The lowest fertility rate occurred in 2000, at 1.49 children per woman.

Fertility in the United States

Based on a June 2004 U.S. Census Bureau study on the Fertility of American Women, in the baby-boom era of the 1950s, the United States recorded its highest fertility rate at 3.5. Fertility rates dropped to their lowest levels, at 1.8 births per woman, in the 1970s. The 2004 data showed an increase in the fertility rate since the millennium, wavering around the 2.0 and 2.10 mark per woman.

Fertility Rates Around the World (2008 estimates from the CIA)

☛ The highest fertility rate is an estimated 7.34 births per woman in Mali, followed closely by Niger at 7.29.

☛ The fertility rate worldwide is 2.58.

☛ The United States sits at 2.10.

☛ The United Kingdom sits at 1.66.

☛ Asian countries register the lowest fertility rates, with Hong Kong the lowest at 1.00.

The C-Section Dilemma

Statisticians have noted what the medical world calls a disturbing finding in birthing trends. It appears that more and more mothers are delivering their babies by cesarean section. While the World Health Organization (WHO) suggests that no more than 15 percent of all newborns should be delivered by this method, in 2005 and 2006, 26 percent of all Canadian newborns were delivered by C-section. Although that number seems high, stats dating back to 2004 for both the U.S. and Australia are even higher, at 29 percent.

Making the Choice for Cesarean

Various birthing techniques and advances in modern medicine have significantly eased the pain of childbirth and have lowered the mortality rate of women in labor. But modern couples are taking it a step further and are opting out of vaginal births altogether in favor of having C-sections. According to the article "Choosy Mothers Choose Cesareans" by Alice Park of *Time* magazine, 31 percent of live births in the U.S. are C-sections. "Around the world, the procedure is becoming even more common: in certain hospitals in Brazil, fully 80 percent of babies are delivered by cesarean." Some studies indicate that of the C-sections being performed, between 4 and 18 percent of them are done based on personal choice and not for medical reasons.

Where's the Money?

The Canadian Council on Social Development reported the estimated cost of raising a child to adulthood in 2004 in this country—and it ain't cheap. According to their numbers, it costs an average of $166,549 to raise a girl to the age of independence (18) and $166,972 to raise a boy to the same age—after all, boys do eat a little more! Using those figures, it'll cost you more than $10,000 to get to your child's first birthday. They also suggest that despite the fact extra-curricular activities and other expenses seem to increase as your child hits the double-digits, it's actually the first five years of a child's life that appear to be the most costly.

DID YOU KNOW?

The National Center for Health Statistics, reported 4,138,349 babies were born in the U.S. in 2005. Canadian figures are considerably lower, with Statistics Canada reporting 346,082 babies born in 2005–06.

BREAKING INTO THE RECORD BOOKS

It's one thing to look at the numbers. They are, after all, only numbers. But what about the little creations behind them? Just a cursory glance through the development of a fetus is enough to convince even the most pessimistic among us that birthing a healthy baby is nothing short of a miracle. Weighing in at an average of 7.6 pounds and having all their fingers and toes is amazing enough, but every once in a while, a baby story pops up that demands just a little more attention.

World's Smallest Surviving Baby

In September 2004, Rumaisa Rahman set a world record. The baby girl, born in Chicago, was 8.6 ounces at birth—and against all odds, she survived. Rumaisa was one half of a set of twins delivered by emergency C-section at just 26 weeks gestation. Her fraternal sister, Hiba, weighed one pound, four ounces at birth and was discharged from the hospital in January 2005. Rumaisa followed her home the next month, making this miracle baby the smallest known surviving baby in the world—a statistic that earned her a place in the *Guinness Book of Records*.

In 2007, Kimberly Mueller came close to breaking that record. This little one was born at 25 weeks gestation and weighed 10 and a half ounces. Doctors rated her chances of surviving at less than 1000 to one, but not only did she survive, she thrived. After six months in the hospital, Kimberly went home. At that point in time, the Mueller baby had the distinction of being the smallest and youngest baby to be born and survive in Germany.

Lightest Triplets

On November 30, 1998, the Coffey family of Virginia welcomed three mini-miracles into the world: Peyton, Blake and Jackson. Although the birth of triplets isn't uncommon, these three babies were a bit of anomaly. Together, the two brothers and one sister weighed only slightly over 3 pounds. The triplets were delivered by C-section—and survived. That rather impressive feat earned them a spot in the *Guinness Book of Records* as the lightest triplets to ever survive.

Shortest Gestation

Another mega-miracle baby is Florida's Amillia Sonja Taylor. This bundle of defiance was born on October 24, 2006—21 weeks and six days after she was conceived in her mother's womb via in vitro fertilization. Amillia weighed 10 ounces, measured 9½ inches in length and wasn't expected to survive. She went home in February 2007, making her the youngest preemie to survive. Prior to Amillia's birth, there were no records of a preemie under 23 weeks gestation surviving.

Three Times Lucky

Jenna Cotton, of Marysville, Ohio, should maybe think about playing the lottery. The mother of three—sons Ayden and Logan and daughter Kayla—made her life easy as far as hosting family birthdays go, anyways. Although the siblings are not triplets, they were all born on October 2—Ayden in 2003, Logan in 2006 and Kayla in 2007.

According to a *Wall Street Journal* article released just after Kayla's birth, number crunchers who enjoy doing this sort of thing figured out that the odds of such an occurrence are a "7.5-in-a-million shot, or one in 133,000."

Heaviest Birth Weight

According to the *Guinness Book of Records*, Anna Haining Swan of Nova Scotia delivered the heaviest baby ever born in Canada. The giant of a woman, who towered a full 7 feet, 5½ inches in height, gave birth to a baby boy on January 19, 1879—weighing in at just under 24 pounds. Although sources aren't clear on the matter, descriptions of Anna's prolonged labor and the struggle doctors had while using forceps and even a "bandage" wrapped around the baby's neck to assist in the delivery suggest he was born naturally. Sadly, the boy only lived for 11 hours. This was the second child born to Anna and her husband of equally impressive stature, Captain Martin Van Buren Bates. The couple's first child, a baby girl, reputedly weighed 18 pounds when she was stillborn on May 19, 1872. At her own birth, Anna herself also weighed 18 pounds. Her parents were both of average height, as were the rest of the couple's 13 children.

A Few Additional Heavyweights

☛ Although some sources refer to the Haining Swan baby as the heaviest ever born, other sources disagree. Several media reports suggest the record holder in this category was born in Effingham, Illinois, in 1939 and weighed a hair less than 30 pounds (29.25 pounds, to be exact). The baby only survived for two hours.

☛ The *Guinness Book of Records* points to Aversa, Italy, when it comes to the heaviest surviving newborn. Carmelina Fedele's son was born in September 1955 and weighed an amazing 22 pounds, 8 ounces. There is, reputedly, another case of a healthy baby born at this weight in 1982, but details are vague.

☛ In January 2005, the Brazilian Gynecological Association reported that country's heaviest newborn. Baby boy Ademilton dos Santos weighed 17 pounds when he made his grand entry. He was the fifth child born to Francisca Ramos dos Santos, but by far the largest. All her other babies were considered "normal weight" babies.

☛ First place for the heaviest combined twin birth weight is believed to go to Mary Ann Ward Haskin of Arkansas. On February 20, 1924, records show she delivered 14-pound Patricia Jane and her brother, 13-pound, 12-ounce John Prosser. Together, the twins weighed a total of 27 pounds, 12 ounces. It must have felt pretty good stepping off the scale after that delivery!

☛ Mary Ann Ward Haskin also earned top spot when it came to birthing the heaviest twin on record. At 14 pounds, that honor goes to her daughter Patricia Jane.

☛ British mom Beth Ryder delivered the heaviest set of fraternal twins on record in that country in October 2007. At a birth weight of 10 pounds, 9 ounces, Theo outweighed his baby sister Millie by a considerable margin. She was a fairly average 8 pounds, 3 ounces at birth.

Youngest Birth Mother

Medical history was made in Peru in 1939 when a young girl arrived at the hospital with what her parents believed were symptoms of an abdominal tumor. It turned out that Lina Medina, who was just five years, seven months and 21 days old, was a month shy of being ready to deliver a full-term baby. Her baby boy was delivered by C-section in May of that year. Just who fathered the child was never disclosed, but her father was initially arrested as a suspect. He was released from custody because of a lack of evidence, and the child was raised as Lina's brother. The boy was 10 when he discovered that his sister was actually his mother.

Oldest Birth Mother

It seems several women are vying for the position of oldest woman in the world to give birth. And the most recent senior mother has given the media the most to talk about. The Spanish woman, Maria del Carmen Bousada Lara, delivered twin boys— Christian and Pau—by cesarean on December 29, 2006. Maria turned 67 seven days later. One of the biggest criticisms of senior women having babies is that they may not live long enough to raise their children to adulthood. Maria likely wasn't worried about that because she was healthy when she received in vitro fertilization. And if longevity runs in families, her own mother—who passed away in 2005 at the ripe old age of 101— was certainly a good measuring stick when Maria pondered her own mortality. Sadly, news reports toward the end of 2007 suggested that she had been recently diagnosed with a serious illness. Although Maria didn't detail her diagnosis, she responded to curious reporters by saying she was receiving treatment and was optimistic about the future.

Other Senior Mothers

☞ Lack of a birth certificate makes this claim hard to prove, but rumor has it that an Indian woman holds the title of the world's oldest birth mother. On June 27, 2008, Omkari Panwar and her husband Charam Singh welcomed fraternal twins—a boy and a girl, each weighing two pounds—into the world. The couple had already raised two daughters and had five grandchildren, but they were desperate to have a male heir. So they spent all the money they had and then some, taking out a bank loan to make up the difference, and traveled north to the state of Uttar Pradesh to undergo in vitro fertilization. "Now, we are very grateful to God, who has answered our prayers," 77-year-old Charam Singh told BBC reporters. While Omkari doesn't have a birth certificate, she claims she was nine years old in 1947, when the British left India. If you do the math, that would have made her a septuagenarian when she gave birth. Although that might make her the world's oldest birth mother, she really doesn't care. She's just grateful for a son and wants to get busy raising the babies "while she is able."

☞ In January 2005, another woman had an earlier claim to being the oldest woman to give birth. A Romanian woman named Adriana Iliescu claimed to be 66 years old when she delivered baby Eliza-Maria by cesarean, six weeks early. Eliza-Maria was one of a set of twin girls, but sadly her sister did not survive. Adriana had been undergoing fertility treatments since she was 58 years old, and this birth came after two failed pregnancies.

☞ The oldest woman in the world to give birth prior to Adriana and Maria was Satyabhama Mahapatra. In 2003, the 65-year-old retired schoolteacher from Nayagarh, India, delivered a baby boy by cesarean. In an interesting side note, Satyabhama and her husband, Krishnachandra, celebrated 50 years of marriage before they welcomed this baby, their first, into the world. The baby was conceived through in vitro fertilization, using the egg and sperm of Satyabhama's niece and her husband. While the cost of such a procedure in Europe or the West can cost tens of thousands of dollars, the Mahapatras paid about 30,000 rupees, or $630.

☛ Britain's oldest birth mother certainly wasn't a stranger to controversy when she delivered a healthy baby boy, nicknamed "JJ," in July 2006 by cesarean. Patricia Rashbrook faced public criticism when it became known that the prominent child psychologist—who was either 62 or 63 years old, depending on the source—was expecting. Patricia and her second husband, John Farrant, bravely withstood the harsh condemnation. Public opinion said the couple were too old, but they firmly believed they were healthy, strong prospective parents and, should anything untoward happen, they had a strong support system in place to care for their baby. Patricia had three children from a previous marriage, but husband John had not been a father before. The birth of their son was nothing short of a miracle in his eyes.

Waiting to Start a Family

Older women looking to have a baby aren't as rare as you might think. According to one statistic from the Human Fertilization and Embryology Authority (HFEA), in 2002, as many as 24 babies were born to women aged 50 or older in the United Kingdom after they went through in vitro fertilization treatment. In 1992, there was only one such birth recorded.

The trend of choosing to parent later in life can be seen in the number of women aged 45 to 49 who opt for IVF treatment, according to the HFEA research. In 1992, women in that age bracket birthed 15 babies, and in 2002, that number increased to 106.

DID YOU KNOW?

The oldest woman thought to have conceived naturally was 57-year-old Ruth Kistler of Portland, Oregon. She gave birth to a baby girl on October 18, 1956.

The Magic of Eight

Eight is considered a lucky number for the Chinese, and although Mel Byrne of Liverpool isn't of that background, her Chinese midwife Bea Fung drew her attention to the belief. You see, there were a whole lot of "eights" involved in the birth of Byrne's baby girl, Lulu. She was born on August 8, 2007, at 8:08 AM after eight hours of labor. To add to the string of lucky numbers, Fung had assisted in eight deliveries that same day. The only thing that would have made the scenario any sweeter was if Lulu had been born a year later. Either way, Fung believes the baby is one lucky little girl—and Fung was just as lucky to be there for the birth!

Quick Turnaround

Jayne Bleackley of New Zealand didn't give her body much chance to recover from the birth of her son, Joseph Robert, on September 3, 1999, before adding to her young family. She gave birth to a daughter on March 30, 2000, which meant baby number two was born less than seven months after Joseph. Jayne entered the *Guinness Book of Records* as the woman with the shortest time span between births.

DID YOU KNOW?

According to a survey conducted by the National Center for Health Statistics in 2003, the month in which most babies are born in the U.S. is July (364,266 babies). February is the month with the lowest number of babies born (307,248). The survey also discovered that more babies were born on Tuesday, and Sunday was the day of the week having the least number of babies born.

Multiple Miracles

Between 1725 and 1765, Mrs. Feodor Vassilyev made world history for having the largest number of children—a record that stands to this day. The woman, who lived in Shuya, Russia, delivered 69 children from 27 pregnancies. Each of those pregnancies resulted in a multiple birth: 16 twins, seven triplets and four quadruplets. Sixty-seven of her children survived. Talk about hitting the record books in a big way!

Taking Some Time

I'm the middle child of three children. Twelve years separate me and my oldest sibling, and there are six years between my younger sibling and me. I thought my mom and dad took their time having us, but apparently, other folks have waited longer— much longer—before providing their child with a sibling.

The *Guinness Book of Records* reports Elizabeth Ann Buttle of Wales waited 41 years and 185 days between the birth of her daughter, Elizabeth Ann, on May 19, 1956, and the birth of her son Joseph on November 20, 1997. She was 60 years old when she had her second child!

The Greatest Gift—Twice Over

Vanderbilt University Hospital in Nashville, Tennessee, reported that Barbara Brennan gave birth to twins in April 2004—a boy named Pryce Daly and a girl named Meredith Taylor. While the birth of twins is certainly a celebration, the birth of these youngsters was doubly so. You see, Brennan is actually the twins' maternal grandmother—she carried and birthed the babies for her daughter, Lynne Bevins, and son-in-law Phil.

The 53-year-old grandmother offered to act as a surrogate shortly after Lynne gave birth to her son Parker and had to undergo an emergency hysterectomy. It took six years before Lynne and Phil decided they'd accept Brennan's offer. Lynne still had her ovaries, so no outside donor was required for the fertilization, and Brennan was simply used as a vessel so that Parker would have a sibling. As luck would have it, he was blessed with two.

DID YOU KNOW?

Jack Nicholson was born on April 22, 1937, in Manhattan, New York City, and called Ethel May his mother and June his sister. It wasn't until *Time* magazine prepared a detailed biography on the actor, who was 37 years old at the time, that Nicholson learned Ethel was in fact his grandmother and June his mother. Both women had already passed away when the secret was revealed.

Longest Period of Gestation

There's been a long-standing urban legend that Hollywood actor Jackie Chan was nestled comfortably in his mother's womb for

12 months. It makes for a good story, but there's no documentation to substantiate the story. However, if a *Time* magazine article, dated March 5, 1945, can be believed, the Chan story might just be true. Mrs. Beulah Hunter, aged 25, reportedly gave birth to a bouncing baby girl after being pregnant for 375 days. Dr. Daniel Beltz confirmed the birth. He stated that on March 24 of the previous year, a pregnancy test he administered to Mrs. Hunter came back positive, and that his patient claimed her last period was on February 10. Still, when she made her grand entry, baby Penny Diana weighed an ounce less than 7 pounds. Some critics of the story suggest that Mrs. Hunter may have unknowingly miscarried a first baby, and then became pregnant immediately afterwards. Since the normal length of a pregnancy is 280 days, it seems a likely possibility.

Twins, You Say?

Most pregnant women give birth to just one baby, but multiple births aren't all that uncommon. Statistics show an average of three percent of pregnancies result in the birth of twins. There are three kinds of twins: identical or monozygotic (same DNA from mother and father in the single egg and single sperm), fraternal or dizygotic (two separate eggs fertilized by the same sperm) and semi-identical (when one egg is fertilized by two separate sperm). The chances of having twins increases if twins run in your family, if you already have a set of twins, and with a woman's age—the older a woman is when she gets pregnant, the higher her chances of having a multiple birth. In 2000 alone, 118,916 sets of twins were born in the United States. About 25 percent of those were identical twins.

Other Twinning Fun Facts

☞ Twins are rarely carried for a full 40-week gestation period. They are most often born around the 37-week mark.

☞ One source states that there are an estimated 125 million twins and triplets in the world. About 10 million of these are monozygotic or identical twins.

☛ England's Louise Brown made medical history on July 25, 1978, when she was born. She was the world's first test-tube baby.

☛ On March 24, 2008, New York City's *Daily News* reported that the first test-tube twins born in the United States had turned 25 years old. Heather and Todd Tilton II were conceived after their parents had tried for six years to have a baby. In vitro fertilization was breakthrough technology at the time, and the couple availed themselves of the medical opportunity. Since the introduction of in vitro fertilization, the occurrence of twin births and other multiple pregnancies has increased by 70 percent in the United States alone.

☛ Scientists estimate that as many as one in eight pregnancies start out as twins, but one twin dies or fails to develop. This phenomenon is called "vanishing twin syndrome."

☛ By far, the least common twin birth is that of conjoined twins—babies who are joined by some part of their bodies at birth. Also known as Siamese twins (so nicknamed because of Chang and Eng Bunker who were born in 1811 in a country that was then known as Siam), the actual occurrence of conjoined twins is not well recorded

☛ Depending on the source, estimates vary of how often conjoined twins occur. The general agreement is that about one in 50,000 pregnancies results in conjoined twins, but most of these fetuses die in utero. The birth of live conjoined twins is thought to occur only once in every 200,000 live births.

☛ All conjoined twins are identical.

☛ A parasitic twin is a part of a vanishing or partially conjoined twin that seemingly grew incompletely from the body of a surviving twin.

☛ Chances of miscarriage are higher with identical twins. On average, it's not uncommon for 20 percent of fraternal twin pregnancies to result in the miscarriage of one fetus.

☛ In some cultures, such as the Balinese, twins of opposite sex were perceived to have had sexual relations in utero and therefore should marry one another later in life. The Mohave tribe of Native Americans, on the other hand, thought opposite sex twins had already married in heaven.

DID YOU KNOW?

Chances of having multiple births are rare, regardless the number of babies expected. However, the odds of birthing all the multiples a pregnant mother might be carrying decreases as the number of fetuses she is carrying increases. According to one source, there's only a one in 8100 chance of giving birth to natural (not a product of fertility treatments) triplets, a one in 729,000 chance of birthing natural quads, and one in 55,000,000 of having natural quintuplets. Add an identical component to the equation, and the odds are greatly increased. For example, giving birth to natural and identical quadruplets is one in 600 million, according to some sources.

AGE-OLD MIRACLE

Life. There's nothing more amazing than the creation of life. That a child is conceived, a fetus develops and a baby is born is nothing short of a miracle. A gazillion evolutions have to take place during a baby's gestation period—and they have to occur EXACTLY—in order for your perfect bundle of joy to appear nine months later. And yet, all things being normal, that's precisely what will happen. Despite any horror stories you might come across, most babies come out just fine. Isn't it wonderful!

How to Get There

If you want to get pregnant, the medical world suggests you allow yourself a three-month rest period after you stop taking oral birth control pills. This gives your body a chance to get back to "normal"—and it also gives you a good chunk of time to practice up! After that, it's no holds barred. If you're among the majority of the female population, you should be pregnant within a year. About 25 percent of women conceive within the first month of trying.

FYI
Just in case you were wondering, no "rest period" is needed between the time you stop using other types of birth control and start trying for a baby.

Boy or Girl?

So, you're planning to have a baby, but not just any baby will do. You want to aim for a specific sex. Although you have a 50-50 shot of having either a boy or girl, there are a number of "methods" available that attempt to determine when you're ovulating or, in layperson's terms, when your body is releasing an egg.

And knowing when you ovulate can help in determining the sex of your baby. The most popular method used to discover when you ovulate is by charting your temperature throughout the month. Your temperature will usually increase a degree or two during ovulation.

Other methods of checking to see if you're getting close to ovulation include a lot of labor-intensive activities that can become a little messy. Thankfully, medical technology has come a long way in the almost three decades since I conceived my first youngster, and now you can buy these newly developed ovulation kits.

The theory behind all this tracking is that if you want a girl, and you know when you're going to be ovulating, you should have intercourse a day or two ahead of this time. That's because—as we all know and if we didn't, we know now—your partner's sperm decides the sex of a baby and female-charged sperm are a little slower than their male counterparts. If you're aiming for a girl and time it right, the male sperm will die off before you ovulate and the female sperm will be pulling up the rear.

If you're going all out in a desperate attempt to have a baby, period, and you've had intercourse during or just before ovulation, chances are pretty good you'll conceive a boy. That's because male-charged sperm are faster and they make the trip to their destination in no time, leaving the female sperm behind. Of course, they're also not as strong and many of them die off more quickly, too. You'll never really know if you've managed to make a boy or a girl until the big day—but you had a lot of fun trying, didn't you?

Witnessing a Miracle

Fathers have been coaching their partners through labor and delivery in the developed world since the mid-1960s, but the practice has been gaining increasing support over subsequent decades. Iranian fathers had their first experience in hospital delivery rooms in 2007. In July, Tehran's Sarem Hospital was the first in that part of the world to allow daddy watch his child's birth. The move to include fathers in the delivery room was the result of a request from Iran's health ministry to reduce the number of cesarean births in that country. It was believed that having hubby around would comfort the laboring mother.

Incidentally, an estimated 70 percent of babies in that country were born by cesarean section. Stats aren't in yet on whether or not the move has made a difference, and truth be told, there's still a lot of debate going on in the rest of the world on whether it's a good thing for dads to be on hand or not. In some cases, fathers are excessively nervous and only add to the tension, giving the laboring mother another thing to worry about—and that's the last thing she needs.

GETTING TO KNOW THE LINGO

If you're planning to get pregnant, or have already tested positive, it's an absolute necessity to brush up on all the lingo doctors and nurses will be throwing at you on the day you deliver. If you don't, you might feel a little like you've gone to sleep and woken up on another planet.

Active Labor

So you've been breathing through contractions for the last dozen hours or more. It's pretty intense, so you think you should check yourself into the hospital. That's when some clever-looking and, you can't help but notice, extremely thin nurse examines you and says you're just one or two centimeters dilated. "That," she informs you, "isn't even active labor." You're just about to give her a pointer or two on childbearing when the doctor arrives and confirms the assessment. A woman isn't considered to be in "active labor" until she's between four and eight centimeters dilated and the contractions are between three and five minutes apart.

Amnion and Amniotic Fluid

Something human mothers share with reptiles, birds and mammals is the development of a membranous sac somewhere around the second week of pregnancy. The sac is actually snug against the growing fetus until it begins to fill with amniotic fluid, which is composed, according to medical journals, of proteins, carbohydrates, lipids and phospholipids, urea and electrolytes—everything the fetus needs to grow. The fluid's chemical makeup changes in the latter stages of pregnancy, when the majority of it is composed of fetal urine.

Apgar Score

It's no surprise that life outside the womb is very different from the snug, cozy surroundings baby was accustomed to. It's quite a shock, actually, and all newborns react a little differently when they are born. To ensure baby is adjusting fine, some of the health-care professionals swarming your room throughout the birth are there to check what's called the Apgar score. Simply put, the medical team will check out your baby's appearance (skin color), pulse, grimace (reflex irritability), activity (muscle tone and movement) and respiration—hence the acronym APGAR. There are different scores for different criteria. For example, if the baby doesn't move when doctors stimulate him or her, the baby will be scored a zero in that category. Some movement is scored one point, and if the baby reacts strongly, a score of two points is given. The most a baby can score is 10, but that isn't typical. Most babies score in the seven-point range.

DID YOU KNOW?

Dr. Virginia Apgar of the U.S. developed this widely used method of scoring newborns in 1952.

Baby Blues

If you've ever been pregnant—or known a pregnant woman—you might notice a tendency towards having a few mood swings. Sometimes there might be a deluge of inexplicable tears and at other times excessive joy. We women tend to blame these mood swings on hormones—and hold onto your hats boys, because we have the scientific data to back that up! Among the many hormonal changes that a woman's body goes through is the secretion of the human chorionic gonadotrophin (HCG). Because the placenta produces this hormone, the only time you'll find it in a woman's body is when she's pregnant. HCG can be detected in both urine and blood tests, so next time your gentle, sweet, pregnant partner takes a crying spell, just blame it on the HCG.

Because of all these hormonal changes going on in a woman's body, it's not uncommon for her to feel a little blue or melancholy after the baby is born. Not only that, you've just spent at least nine months gearing up for this grand finale, and it's finally here. It's a little like the first day of a new year or the day after your wedding—most of us feel a little bit down, even though we're also thrilled and excited about what lies ahead. So don't beat yourself up for feeling a little blue. Do discuss it with your doctor, though. In some cases baby blues can develop into depression, also known as "postpartum distress syndrome," but this, too, isn't outside the norm.

Baby Farming

If you think this term sounds derogatory, you're right. The nicest possible definition of the term is that it was, in a very broad way, a precursor to daycare, but that is more than a little deceiving. Historically, a woman being paid to breastfeed and care for an unrelated child was referred to as a baby farmer. Although, in some instances, this was a practice of convenience for the baby's family, most of the time the children being farmed out to other families were illegitimate, and their mothers found work to pay their expenses. (If you're familiar with Victor Hugo's masterpiece *Les Misérables*, the character Cosette was left in this situation while her mother worked long hours to support her.)

Bloody Show

"Bloody Hell?" you think as you notice a pink stain on your underwear. At first you're annoyed, arguing that being pregnant means not having to deal with this kind of inconvenience until baby is born. Then you might get concerned that something is wrong—spotting, generally speaking, isn't a good thing when you're pregnant. However, if you're near your due date, this bloody show might be a sign your body is getting ready to go into labor. In any case, you should consult your doctor.

Braxton Hicks

Braxton Hicks contractions are uterine cramps that might feel like labor pains but aren't. While not every pregnant woman experiences these contractions, they are quite common and can begin as early as week six for some very unlucky women. Thankfully, most moms-to-be won't feel them until much later in their pregnancy, and for those of you who are plagued by these pre-labor pains, changing positions or taking a warm bath may ease the pain. Another suggestion is to drink a glass of water—you could be dehydrated.

DID YOU KNOW?

Braxton Hicks contractions were named after John Braxton Hicks, the British doctor who discovered them in 1872.

Breech Presentation

In a perfect world, all babies would arrive head down in the pelvis and face to the floor. When a baby is delivered with bum, arms, legs or some other configuration of body parts first, this is considered a breech presentation. If you average out all the breech deliveries, you'd discover that between three and four percent of all babies are born this way. However, most of those deliveries occur when the baby is born early. WebMD suggests that breech deliveries occur 25 percent of the time in births prior to 28 weeks' gestation, about seven percent at 32 weeks' gestation and one to three percent of births at term.

Types of Breech Presentations

☞ Frank breech—Baby is in the "pike position," basically bum first with both legs extended to the head. This is the most common form of breech presentation, occurring in between 50 and 70 percent of births.

☞ Complete breech—Baby is in the "cannonball position," with hips and knees flexed. This happens in 5–10 percent of breech births.

☞ Incomplete breech—Baby isn't sure whether to do the cannonball or pike, and one leg is bent while the other is extended. This happens in 10–30 percent of breech births.

Cervix
The neck-shaped opening to the uterus.

Colostrum

The fluid expressed through the nipple before a mother's milk supply is established. This first milk, or "foremilk," contains sugar, protein, minerals and antibodies vital to the baby's health.

Cone Heads

No, I'm not talking about the *Saturday Night Live* skit that propelled the development of an animated movie and another with real people in it in the 1980s and 1990s. I'm talking about the oddly shaped skull some babies have when born. It's not uncommon for babies, especially those who have spent a long time in the birth canal, to emerge with a slightly elongated skull because of the malleability of a newborn's bones. In medical terms, the end result is called "molding," but the rest of us just call it "cone head."

Dilation
The opening of the cervix in preparation for birth. Dilation occurs as the baby makes its way down the birth canal and is measured in terms of centimeters. Once mama's cervix measures 10 centimeters, she's usually ready to deliver that bundle of joy!

DID YOU KNOW?

Although dilation of the cervix usually means it's time for baby to arrive, some women can be two or three centimeters dilated for several days before active labor starts.

Dizygotic Twins
The result of two separate eggs (*di* means "two," and *zygotic* means "ova" or "egg") fertilized at the same time. Dizygotic twins are also known as "fraternal twins."

Doula

The original Greek meaning of the word *doula* is "woman of service," or even "slave," but doula has a much deeper meaning today. It refers to a person who is trained in the art of assisting in childbirth.

Due Date

Theoretically, a baby's birth date is calculated by counting 40 weeks from the first day of a woman's last period. Of course, babies tend to come when they want to, and statistics show that about 85 percent arrive sometime within one week before and one week after that magic "due date."

Ectopic Pregnancy

An ectopic pregnancy happens when an egg is fertilized some-where other than in the uterine cavity. Ninety-eight percent of the time, this occurs in the fallopian tubes, hence the nickname "tubal pregnancy." However, an ectopic pregnancy can also happen in the cervix, ovaries and abdomen. In most cases, the woman will miscarry the baby because the area of fertilization doesn't have the space needed to nurture a growing fetus. If for some reason the woman doesn't miscarry, medical intervention is often required because this kind of pregnancy cannot develop to term and is often dangerous to the woman's health.

DID YOU KNOW?

On rare occasions, a woman who has had a hysterectomy can experience an ectopic pregnancy.

Embryo

This is the term given to a fertilized egg during the first eight weeks after it has implanted in a woman's uterus.

Episiotomy

It's not uncommon for small tears to occur at the bottom of a woman's vagina during childbirth, but if a doctor is concerned about the direction the tear might take—for example, into the anus—the doctor might make a surgical incision called an episiotomy in the area to lessen the chance of damage.

Fetus

Once the embryo has survived eight weeks, and until the actual birth, the little creation is referred to in the medical world as a fetus.

Freebirth

This is a birth that occurs without any assistance from a doctor or a trained doula or midwife.

Gravida

Gravida is a Latin term that refers to the number of times a woman has been pregnant.

Jaundice

This is a condition that occurs when large amounts of bilirubin are produced in the liver. A newborn's skin might turn a little yellow, along with the whites of the eyes. This isn't altogether uncommon. Sometimes it takes a while before a newborn's liver is able to process the extra amount of red blood cells it no longer needs now that it has entered the world outside the uterus, and some of the excess pigment (the yellow bilirubin) causes the visible discoloration. Some babies just need additional breastfeeding to flush the bilirubin out of their systems while others might need to spend some time under phototherapy lights. Jaundice usually disappears around the fourth day after birth. On occasion, the condition can be a sign of something more serious. Either way, a visit to your doctor is in order.

Kick Count

Prenatal care has come a long way since I've had my babies. Today, along with eating healthy, getting a lot of rest and exercise, pregnant women have another chore to conduct on a fairly regular basis. Most moms-to-be can feel baby kicking somewhere between the 18- and 25-week mark—closer to the 25-week mark if this is a first pregnancy, and earlier for subsequent pregnancies.

Once it's clear that's a kick you feel and not gas, your doctor will probably ask you to keep track of your baby's kick count. Simply put, once you determine the time of day your baby is usually active, set aside some time to count the movements. This helps ascertain your baby's particular pattern, and any radical change from that pattern should be reported to your doctor.

Lotus Birth

Also known as "umbilical nonseverance," a Lotus birth allows baby and placenta to remain attached for a period of time following the birth. Practitioners of Lotus birthing argue that this natural birthing practice encourages immediate bonding between the mother and newborn, rather than delaying that bond with the usual hospital practice of whisking junior off for suctioning and assessment. Some practitioners also believe that a Lotus birth allows baby to receive all the nutrient-rich blood from the placenta. Within 5 to 10 minutes, a mucus-like substance called Wharton's jelly (named after Thomas Wharton, the English doctor who first identified it) thickens inside the cord, naturally separating baby and placenta, and the cord will naturally fall off within 2 to 10 days.

Depending on how far the parents are interested in taking this practice, the clamping of the cord can be delayed for just a few minutes or altogether. In the case where parents want the cord to detach by itself, which is a full Lotus birth, the attached placenta is placed in a bowl near the baby until that occurs.

This birthing practice was named after Clair Lotus Day, a California woman who questioned the medical practice of cutting the umbilical cord when she was pregnant in 1974. She managed to find a doctor sympathetic to her beliefs, and she took her newborn son Trimurti home from the hospital still attached to his placenta. The World Health Organization suggests that late clamping is the physiological (natural) way to go in a normal pregnancy and birth, and when the hormone oxytocin has not been used to stimulate contractions. According to one source, the only example of this practice in the animal kingdom occurs in chimpanzees.

Milk Siblings

Milk siblings are unrelated babies who are breastfed by another child's mother. In some cultures where the use of a wet nurse is prevalent, these children develop a unique bond to each other and to the woman breastfeeding them.

Miscarriage
A miscarriage is the spontaneous birthing of an embryo or fetus long before it's ready for life outside the uterus. Usually this happens in the first 20 weeks of pregnancy, and the risk of having

a miscarriage decreases as a pregnancy passes that milestone. If birth occurs shortly after the 20-week mark, it's considered a premature birth or, if the baby doesn't survive, a stillbirth. On rare occasions, a woman's body doesn't automatically react as it should when a pregnancy fails. This is called a "missed miscarriage" and can be diagnosed by an ultrasound, which is scheduled because the doctor hasn't noticed any growth of the fetus.

Mittelschmerz

Some women experience slight pain in the lower abdominal and pelvic region during ovulation. This is called *mittelschmerz*, a German word meaning "middle pain." About 20 percent of women are believed to experience this pain, though not necessarily with every monthly cycle.

Monozygotic Twins
Otherwise known as identical twins, monozygotic twins (*mono* means "one," and *zygotic* means "ova" or "egg") occur when a single egg divides after fertilization. In most cases, these twins have almost identical DNA.

Morning Sickness

Hyperemesis gravidarum, another term for morning sickness, usually occurs during the first three months, or first trimester, of a pregnancy. In fact, frequent trips to the bathroom to vomit before you've even had your morning coffee, which for some reason even the smell of now sends your stomach into somersaults, is often the first telltale sign that you might be pregnant. Of course, you can experience "morning sickness" at any time of the day, you lucky girl you. The good news is that it usually disappears somewhere around the 13-week mark. On the other hand, a few women will struggle with nausea and vomiting throughout their entire pregnancy. Some women have luck managing it by eating small, frequent meals, staying away from spicy foods, sucking on hard candy or wearing an acupuncture wrist band.

DID YOU  KNOW?

Fraternal twins develop in their own separate placentas, but identical twins share the same placenta.

Mucus Plug

So by now you're likely well aware that some vaginal discharge nearing your delivery is normal, but you suddenly discover something a little more substantial. The mucus plug blocks the cervical opening, and when it starts to come away, you might notice a thicker, stringier, brownish substance being discharged. In some cases, the mucus plug can be quite thick and almost rubbery in consistency. Release of the mucus plug is usually a sign that you're getting ready to deliver, but don't pack your bags just yet. It could be another week, maybe even two—if you're as lucky as my daughter—before the big day finally arrives.

Para
Para is a Latin term that refers to the number of times a woman has given birth. In this instance, a miscarriage is not considered a birth.

Placenta
The placenta is the organ that lines the uterus and is attached to the growing fetus. After baby is born, the mom feels a few additional contractions, and the placenta, or afterbirth, is expelled.

Quickening
This term is used to describe the first time a pregnant mother feels the baby move. (Baby has been moving all along but prior to this stage was too small for mom to feel those movements.)

Stretch Marks
These nasty little road maps that wind their way around your belly are actually torn parts of the skin caused by excessive stretching during pregnancy. Unfortunately, they're not restricted to the tummy area and can occur on the butt, legs and breasts as well. The other bad news is that contrary to popular belief, stretch marks can't be prevented or completely rectified after they appear. The good news is that they usually fade over time. If it makes you feel better to use the popular cocoa butter and vitamin E creams, go for it. If you're really determined to rid yourself of those pink and purple streaks, consult a dermatologist. Some women have had a modicum of success undergoing cosmetic procedures such as microdermabrasion, pulsed-dye laser therapy and radiofrequency dermal remodeling.

Trimester
Human mothers are pregnant for about 40 weeks, give or take a week or two. This length is divided into three time periods known as the first, second and third trimesters.

Varicose Veins

Stretch marks are just one of the possible side effects of pregnancy. Another is the development of varicose veins. These bluish-purple veins that are suddenly more visible and often elevated from the surface of the skin result from the increased blood flow necessary in pregnancy. Varicose veins are usually confined to the legs but can also pop up, sorry to tell you, in the form of hemorrhoids. Varicose veins can be painful, but wearing support stockings or elevating your legs can sometimes reduce the discomfort.

Vernix

This is the cheesy-white protective covering that develops around the fetus during the second trimester and is often still visible at your baby's birth.

Wet Nurse

I'll bet you can figure out the definition of this phrase. If you guessed that it means a "nurse" or nanny who breastfeeds, you'd be correct. A wet nurse was historically a lactating woman who, for various reasons, was called upon to breastfeed an infant not her own. Sometimes this request came about because the birth mother was ill, had a multiple birth and was having difficulties feeding each of her newborns or was just feeling inadequate to the task. It's interesting to note that women who aren't lactating as a result of a pregnancy are still capable of producing milk, so some wet nurses were not mothers in their own right.

DID YOU KNOW?

A wet nurse was often used by the socially elite who were anxious to produce a male heir. It was believed that a new mother who didn't breastfeed would begin ovulating sooner than a lactating mother would.

TRIMESTER MILESTONES

Although babies are born in all different lengths and weights, certain milestones are uniformly met in most pregnancies.

First Trimester

At two months gestation, your baby-to-be is about the size of a kidney bean and already is managing to have your gut twirling somersaults and your hormones doing head spins. So it might help you to know that after the first trimester, or at about 13 weeks, some progress is actually being made. By then, the fetus will have:

- ☛ a measurement of around 3 inches (9 cm)

- ☛ a weight of about 1.7 ounces (48 grams)

- ☛ arms, legs and a distinct torso and head

- fingers and toes that are starting to form
- distinct fingerprints
- bones that are starting to harden
- a heart rate of about 140 beats per minute
- lungs that "breathe" amniotic fluid
- lips and a mouth that is learning how to suck

DID YOU KNOW?

After the first month of pregnancy, a fetus might only measure a quarter of an inch, but amazing things are already happening within this small body. Blood is flowing through veins, the brain is rapidly developing and will soon be able to coordinate muscle movement, and the baby's heart has been beating for a week now.

Second Trimester

Morning sickness has usually subsided considerably by the time you enter the second trimester, but a woman's body is still working hard to help the baby develop. By the time you've hit the 25-week mark, your baby will:

- weigh between 1½ and 2 pounds and measure somewhere around the 10-inch mark
- be completely formed
- have eyebrows and eyelashes
- have bodily systems that are operational
- form fat under the skin, which means the baby is a little less wrinkly
- have fingernails and toenails that are fully developed

Third Trimester

By now, a mother-to-be is getting really excited about the impending birth of her long-awaited little one, or she's starting to feel like a beached whale. Or, more likely, she's feeling a little of both.

☛ During this trimester, your baby will gain the majority of its weight. It starts out this last phase of development at about the three-pound mark and gains about one-half pound a week until the 37th week. At full term, the average baby weighs 6 to 9 pounds, and measures between 19 and 21 inches.

☛ Usually around the seven-month mark, the baby will already be able to identify mama's voice. Baby can also recognize papa's voice if he speaks to the tummy on a regular basis.

☛ By week 28, the baby can open and close his eyes, and he will seek out and follow light.

☛ Until about the 32nd week of gestation, your baby's body is covered with soft, downy hair called "lanugo." By this point in the pregnancy that hair starts to fall off, and the majority of it disappears within the next two weeks.

☛ While all internal organs are developed by the end of the second trimester, the baby is still growing and gaining strength during the third trimester. According to the Mayo Clinic, it's not until week 30 that baby starts to "practice breathing by moving his or her diaphragm in a repeating rhythm."

WEIRD CRAVINGS 101

Pregnant women craving weird food combinations, such as pickles and ice cream, have been the long-standing joke. But if you've ever been pregnant, you know those cravings aren't something to laugh about—they feel like they're a matter of life and death!

Call it an old wives' tale if you will, but a commonly held belief is that a craving indicates your body is missing something. Even my much older (and wiser) sister supported the merits of this argument. When she was pregnant with her fourth child, she had a rather odd craving—ice. Sometimes her craving was so intense that when she didn't have any ice cubes left, she'd scour her always immaculately cleaned freezer for any residual ice buildup that may have accumulated since her last weekly defrosting (she will quite likely kill me for including this little bit of trivia, or she may deny it altogether).

There is scientific proof that ice contains some levels of sodium and potassium. As a well-educated health-care professional, my sister, of course, knew this and argued that her strange craving was the result of her body lacking these important elements. (One source suggests a strong craving for ice also could be a sign of an iron deficiency.)

Science has yet to definitively prove why cravings tend to be common among pregnant women, but it does seem most moms-to-be experience them to varying degrees. After all, mama's body is working around the clock to produce a healthy offspring, and it isn't unreasonable to think she needs a little replenishing from time to time.

I Need Meat!

Excessive cravings for red meat (which have been reported even among women who are vegetarian) aren't uncommon and could indicate a need for more iron in the diet.

A Dirty Secret?

Feel like eating a cup of dirt or chewing on chalk? The good news is you're not going crazy. Such cravings aren't as strange as you might think, but you should definitely call your doctor. Craving inedible substances such as these can be a sign of an eating disorder known as "pica," which is often found among individuals struggling with malnutrition. It's occasionally experienced during pregnancy and, again, could signify an iron deficiency. It could also indicate the mother is feeling stressed or fearful or physically under the weather, or it could just be a weird tale to share with your child when he or she is older. Either way, resist the urge to consume these non-edibles, because ingesting them could result in anything from a chipped tooth to a bowel obstruction to lead poisoning.

CELEBRITY CRAVINGS

Strange culinary desires aren't simply a struggle for everyday folks like you and I. No, no, no—bigwig superstars are human, too!

Just Ask Brad Pitt

According to one source, when Angelina Jolie was expecting Shiloh, she desperately craved Reese's Pieces. Now, if you recall, the couple was residing in Namibia at the time, where there isn't an overabundance of the peanut butter chocolate treat. So Pitt took matters in his own hands and simply ordered some—a whole crate—direct from Hershey, Pennsylvania. Although craving something like Reese's Pieces isn't all that strange, another celebrity rag states that Jolie's latest cravings, during her 2008 pregnancy, were a little more exotic: French fries dipped in milkshakes and/or hot sauce, and onion rings with mustard and a chocolate chaser. On July 12, Jolie gave birth to twins: Vivienne Marcheline and Knox Leon. There's no word on whether the arrival of her new daughter and son put an end to her odd cravings.

Bone Marrow, You Say?

Ukrainian model and Hollywood actress Milla Jovovich reported craving bone marrow spread on bread during her pregnancy with son Ever Gabo Jovovich Anderson. This might sound strange to folks today, but traditionally the bone marrow of large animals was cooked up and eaten just like the rest of the animal. And eating cooked bone marrow on bread was quite common among certain cultures even just a few decades ago. By the way, baby boy Ever made his grand entry on November 3, 2007. His proud papa is writer-director Paul Anderson.

Sweet and Spicy
Marc Anthony's music diva wife J. Lo reportedly craved salsa and M&Ms with an orange soda chaser. A strange combination for sure, but carrying twins has to have a few fringe benefits!

Never Enough Chocolate
Jenny McCarthy reportedly gained 80 pounds during her pregnancy with baby Evan in 2002. She obviously didn't have too much difficulty ditching the weight after he was born, and hearing about her craving for brownies is somehow comforting.

Tried and True
The old standby, pickles and ice cream, was apparently a favorite for Cate Blanchett during her third pregnancy. Baby boy Ignatius was born on April 13, 2008.

Unlimited Choice
In the British magazine, *Limited Edition*, actress and TV presenter Davina McCall is quoted as saying she craved "sugar, Coca Cola, chewing on ice and gnawing on sponges" during her three pregnancies. "Don't ask," she added. "It must have been something to do with my gums." (Just FYI, Davina has produced the successful and, if fan reports are any indication, very helpful video *Davina: My Pre and Post Natal Workouts*.)

Crunching on Spaghetti
Being married to Food Network favorite Jamie Oliver didn't make former model Juliette Norton's pregnancy cravings more exotic than the next gal's. Jamie's lovely wife reportedly craved Marmite (a vegetable-based food spread) slathered on bananas. She also apparently had a hankering for uncooked spaghetti.

Not That Odd

For a good year you couldn't walk by a grocery newsstand without seeing glossy color covers of Britney Spears ducking from one photographer or another. So this book would be sadly lacking if there weren't at least one reference to the pop diva. According to one source, Britney had an odd pregnancy craving—dirt. As mentioned earlier, and in her defense, the craving for dirt and other "non-edibles" *isn't* something all that out of the ordinary, despite what the celebrity gossip magazines might suggest.

Sweet, Sour, Salty

Imagine this: slices of watermelon enhanced with salt and lime. This was just one of a number of cravings Elisabeth Hasselbeck, of the talk show *The View*, enjoyed during her second pregnancy, and while I've never heard of this one before, you've got to admit it's almost diet-friendly. Taylor Thomas Hasselbeck was born on November 9, 2007.

Talk About Healthy!

Ever heard of *Melrose Place, Ally McBeal* and *According to Jim*? Courtney Thorne-Smith appeared in all three prime-time shows. Courtney became pregnant in 2007, and she had an interesting and healthy craving before birthing baby boy Jacob "Jake" Emerson Fishman on January 11, 2008. One celebrity news outlet mentioned that Courtney craved cottage cheese during her pregnancy.

Radishes Anyone?

Nicole Kidman also reportedly enjoyed a healthy, if not a slightly odd, craving during her pregnancy. It appears that she just couldn't get her fill of radishes.

FOOD EXTRAVAGANZA

So we've all agreed—being pregnant somehow hardwires your brain and belly to make interesting food choices. At the same time, your doctor is weighing you every visit and raising his eyebrows if you're gaining too much or too little weight between visits. Watching your caloric intake and eating healthy doesn't have to be boring. And isn't pregnancy the very best time to try something new? Who knows, you might develop a healthy craving that sticks with you after baby is born.

The Good Old Standby

Remember the saying, "An apple a day keeps the doctor away?" There's good reason for that. Apples are packed with vitamins A and C, iron, calcium and all kinds of goodness. An apple makes a healthy treat, but if you're looking to switch it up a bit, cut it up and slather on a tablespoon of peanut butter. If you prefer a spicier version, sprinkle cinnamon on the sliced apple.

DID YOU KNOW?

Bananas and peanut butter are another favorite combination. Or how about bananas and cream or bananas and yogurt or banana smoothies...

One Sweet Baby

Fans of the Baby Ruth chocolate bar have no doubt heard the urban legend about how the bar, created by the Curtiss Candy Company in the 1920s, was named after President Grover Cleveland's daughter Ruth. The claim was later refuted since the young Ruth Cleveland died in 1904, long before the company even opened its doors in 1916.

Of course because baseball player Babe Ruth was making head-lines for the Boston Red Sox right around the time the bar was introduced, other folks wondered if he was the reason for the name. He wondered too—and his people raised the question with the company. The company, however, denied the charge.

Another explanation of the history behind the name was that it was in honor of Ruth Williamson, the wife of the president of the Williamson Candy Company, a company that was suppos-edly one of the developers behind the new recipe. But since the Williamson Candy Company was a competitor in the industry, this explanation for the name is highly unlikely.

Although there's never been a definitive explanation to the name's origin, the history of the development of the bar itself is a little clearer. According to several sources, the nutty chocolate bar was originally called Kandy Kake. It didn't do as well as the Curtiss Candy Company had hoped, so they made some altera-tions, replaced the original pastry center with a fudge-like nou-gat and rebranded the bar as Baby Ruth. And regardless of how and why it got its name, the bar itself was a success for many decades.

Creamy Alternative
Switch up the ice cream fix with a bowl of vanilla yogurt and your favorite berries.

Crunching on a Cracker
Some sources suggest a salty snack, such as a few crackers, is good for combating nausea during pregnancy. For a little protein boost, why not slather on your favorite flavor of light cream cheese.

Yummy, and Pretty Too!

So you're addicted to chips and dip? Why not trade in the fatty variety of dip for a healthier, low-calorie bruschetta? Finely chop up a tomato, add some sweet red peppers, spice it up with fresh parsley and maybe some crushed garlic or diced onions if spices don't upset your stomach, add a dash of olive oil and a couple of grains of salt and—*voilà*—a low-calorie dip, which means you can indulge in at least a handful of lightly salted taco chips.

No Excuses

Always have a veggie or fruit platter on hand loaded with your favorites. And if you weren't much of a fresh fruit and veggie muncher before you became pregnant, chances are if you indulge in this snack throughout your pregnancy, you will be addicted to it after.

New Twist on Old Favorites

If you've walked through the cereal aisle of your local supermarket lately, you'll notice the newest fad in packaged granola is "sweet and salty." Why not try your own version by adding shelled sunflower seeds, peanuts or other nutty favorites to your yogurt or ice cream fix?

BREAST OR BOTTLE?

While the choice to breastfeed is an intensely personal one, and not all mothers decide to take this route, the World Health Organization (WHO) supports this natural method of feeding newborns. In fact, the WHO suggests that whenever possible, mothers breastfeed until the baby is two years or older. On the other hand, all the benefits of breastfeeding are likely tossed out the window if you are continually struggling to have your baby latch on or you are intensely stressed by the process. Most mothers weigh the pros and cons of either breastfeeding or giving formula to their newborn. Here are just a few thoughts to ponder if you're in that decision-making mode.

The Great Debate

☞ Breastfed newborns eat every two or three hours, while bottle-fed babies are ready for their next feeding of between two and four ounces every three or four hours. In other words, you're looking at a minimum of six feedings in a 24-hour period.

☞ Breastfeeding offers a unique bonding experience for mother and babe, so if you're planning to adopt, and you've always wanted to breastfeed, don't rule out breastfeeding altogether! Given a lead time of at least four months, routine use of an electric breast pump will stimulate milk production. (In fact, men can stimulate milk production and successfully breastfeed—and if you don't believe me, just check it out on the Internet.) Of course, the amount of breast milk produced in either case is usually significantly less than that of a woman who has gone through pregnancy. That means baby will likely need to have breastfeeding supplemented.

☞ And if you're not into washing bottles, breastfeeding is one way to minimize that chore. No bottles involved!

Working with the Body

☞ If cuddling up to baby doesn't result in his latching on, don't fret. There are four different positions suggested to breastfeeding moms, and cradling, with baby's head in the crook of your arm, is just one of them. The others include cross-cradling (supporting baby's head with the opposite hand), the football hold (your baby's feet are tucked under your arm and you're holding the body and head like a football), and lying down.

☞ Breastfeeding causes the new mother's uterus to contract, helping it return to its pre-pregnancy state a lot quicker than if mom doesn't breastfeed.

☞ Breastfeeding often causes the lovely side effect of preventing menstruation. That means the longer you breastfeed, the longer you can be period free.

☞ For some extremely lucky moms, breastfeeding is also a great way to lose weight. (I was never thinner than when I breastfed. Unfortunately, that doesn't mean I stayed that way!)

☞ Breastfeeding is also believed to reduce the risk of developing breast, ovarian, cervical and uterine cancers.

Counting Those Pennies

Since using store-bought, homogenized milk isn't suggested until baby is one year old, breast milk is certainly the more cost-effective option. According to one study, conducted in San Diego in 2001, the cost of using powdered formula was about $99 per month or $1188 per year. Ready-made formula was even more expensive, costing as much as $2376 per year if you use eight-ounce cans sold in a four-pack. Depending on the type of formula you prefer, a hungry, growing newborn can consume about $240 of formula each month, putting a heavy strain on the grocery bill.

Nutrient-rich Food

The medical community calls breast milk an infant's perfect food. In most cases, a baby should receive all the nutrients needed from breast milk alone for the first six months outside the womb.

If you think your little one is a major chomper, and there's no way you'll ever produce enough milk to meet your baby's needs, don't panic. In most cases, the more baby suckles, the more milk you'll produce.

DID YOU KNOW?

Many women with breast implants have successfully breastfed their babies. So if you've had breast implants and want to breast-feed, don't count yourself out quite yet.

Nipple Confusion

Some sources dissuade new mothers who are planning to breast-feed from using soothers or supplementing their breast milk. This is because they believe different nipples can frustrate the baby, who might find it easier to latch onto one nipple over another—some call this "nipple confusion." If the nipple your babe prefers isn't the natural kind, you might find breastfeeding a bit of a struggle. (Of course, there are lots of babies out there who don't ever encounter this problem.)

Spicy Tales

If you're breastfeeding and stop by your grandmother's house for supper, chances are her meal is easy on the spice. That's because it's a long-standing belief (one that every grandmother sub-scribed to) that spicy foods would upset babe's tummy. While that might be the case on occasion, generally speaking anything goes. After all, mothers down in Mexico don't necessarily let up on the hot sauce!

More Convenient than You Thought

Breast milk can be expressed and stored for up to three days in the fridge, two weeks in a fridge freezer and 6 to 12 months in a self-contained deep freeze, which is all good news, especially if you're a mom who works outside the home.

If you don't think breastfeeding is something a strong, career-minded (and a little bit sexy) woman would do, you might be interested to know that some of today's leading ladies in public service and the entertainment industry have breastfed their children. Among them, according to one source, are Hillary Clinton, the late Princess Diana, Sophia Loren, Pamela Anderson, Demi Moore, Faith Hill and Madonna.

Free Cleavage
Moms who breastfeed are naturally enhanced—cleavage-wise.

Word of Caution

The one instance where a mother really needs to question if breastfeeding is the way to go is if she is infected with HIV/AIDS. In this case, the decision whether to breastfeed or not should be discussed with your health-care provider.

DID YOU KNOW?

NBA hotshot Michael Jordan, multiple MVP winner, was breastfed for the first three years of his life. His mother is quoted by one source as saying, "I feel this is why he is the athlete he is."

GETTING TO KNOW THE NEW KID

So you've had the baby and, in today's hospitals, you may feel like you haven't even had a moment's rest before you're signing the discharge papers and and taking baby home. At this point the entire birthing experience might seem little more than a blurred memory, and did you even have the chance to check out if your youngster has all his or her fingers and toes?

Of course, by this time you've welcomed countless visitors, and each one has told you something remarkable about some baby in their lives. If your mother-in-law is anything like mine, you've likely heard how your significant other was potty trained before his first birthday and spoke in full sentences by the age of 18 months. These anomalies do occur, but they aren't the norm, and you shouldn't use them as a measuring stick for your baby's development. Likewise, the milestone moments that follow are only averages. All babies are unique and are on their very own personal journeys.

So don't panic. Moms throughout the ages have felt exactly as you do right now. Instead, enjoy the wonder of your newborn. And check out some of the interesting baby facts that might make you smile.

Nip and Tuck

Once you get a chance to really look at your newborn, you might wonder if the little tyke is ever going to straighten up. Babies look a little tucked and curled, like they can't straighten out quite yet. In fact, they don't actually fully stretch out until they reach the six-month mark.

Shock and Awe

Have you ever sneezed or burped while holding a newborn? If so, you may have noticed him arch his back and swing out his arms and legs—and he might even burst into tears while he's at it. This is called the Moro or startle reflex, one of several strong reflexes babies are born with.

Those Cute Toes!

Another powerful newborn reflex is the Babinski reflex. Try rubbing your baby's bare feet and watch her toes. The big toe will bend upwards, and the other toes will fan out.

Step One, Step Two

Once baby is old enough that you feel comfortable holding him upright, you'll notice he looks like he wants to walk. No, he's not eons ahead of his time. This is a newborn reflex called the step reflex, which is stimulated when the baby's feet touches something firm.

Mealtime Etiquette

When you start feeding your mini-me pablum, usually somewhere around the three-month mark, you'll notice that darlin' baby of yours seems to be using her tongue to push everything you just put into her mouth back out again. Your baby really likes the dinner but is learning how to use the tongue thrust reflex.

Can You See Me Now?

Just how much babies can see during the first few days and weeks of life has been a subject of much debate. Most sources suggest that newborns can actually see about 10 inches in front of them. By the time they're eight months old, their sight is almost what it would be for an adult.

Look at that Smile

At the end of a baby's first month of life, she should be able to life her head and respond to sounds. She'll also laugh or smile and has a little neck control.

Getting Stronger

By month two, baby is getting stronger. Now he can lift his head and his shoulders while on his tummy.

Baby Knows Mama

By the time babies reach their second or third month, not only do they recognize their parents' faces but their voices and scents, too! You might notice that your baby smiles when spoken to, responds to loud noises and seems to have discovered her hands.

The First Tooth

When junior hits four months, he can likely bear some of his weight when you hold him upright on the floor. Teething is always fun about this time, and don't be surprised if he's already cut his first tooth. He's also starting to turn his squeals and baby blabber into sounds such as "mama" and "dada."

DID YOU KNOW?

Every baby is different, and the rule of thumb when it comes to weight gain is that babies should double their birth weight by the age of four months and triple it by their first birthday.

Where Did You Go?
Now that the light in your life recognizes your face, voice and scent, it only makes sense that by the five-month mark your baby is going to start fussing excessively when you're not in her line of vision.

Getting Mobile

The six-month mark sees baby conquering a number of milestones. By this time, your baby is likely rolling over, sitting on his own, grabbing for his toys, trying to talk and possibly even starting to crawl.

Stranger Anxiety
Babies start "making strange" around the six-month mark, but according to a study published by researchers at Yale University in the fall of 2007, that reaction could be a lot more grounded than once thought. The study suggests that by this age, a baby understands something about "social cooperation" and is generally more attracted to folks who are easygoing than individuals who are loud and nasty. I tend to agree with them!

Fine Motor Skills

By six months, your baby's ability to grab and pick up toys is improving. Babies are learning to use their thumb and forefinger to pick up toys, and around this time you'll notice that your baby likes to play with the "toys" you play with, such as a wooden spoon or a metal bowl when you're in the kitchen pre-paring a meal.

That First Step

At the 12-month mark, if baby isn't walking, he's just about ready to. You'll need to have baby gates leading up and down the stairs because he's mighty curious and will want to and be able to climb.

Artist in Training

If you give your little one a package of fat crayons to play with at this stage, don't be surprised that when you turn your back, your home will be redesigned. By this time, babies have enough motor control to hold crayons and scribble, but maybe not enough control to confine themselves to a coloring book!

DID YOU KNOW?

Babies are born without kneecaps. Well, that's not exactly the whole story, but like many urban legends, there is a tiny bit of truth to the matter. Babies are born with kneecaps, but they consist of more cartilage than bone. These "kneecaps" ossify around the three-year mark for girls and at age four or five for boys.

MAKING MOTHERHOOD EASIER

*Birthing and raising babies is a lot of work; there's no
getting around that. But that doesn't mean we shouldn't try
to make life a little less stressful. After all, we wanted a
baby to love and enjoy, not just toil over and find ourselves
exhausted at the end of the day. What follows is a list of
innovative inventions, many created by women, that have
made childrearing much more enjoyable.*

Baby's Best Friend

Baby bottles have been around practically since the dawn of
time. Originally, they were double-spouted—liquid was poured
into one end and expelled at the other. The spout where baby
suckled was hard, similar to the sipping end of a sippy cup.
Although softer materials were tried from time to time, these
types of nipples were hard to keep clean. The first such "feeding
cup" ever discovered, according to Mead Johnson Nutritional
Division, was discovered in Phoenikas, Cyprus. It dates back to
2000 BC and is said to resemble a teapot.

DID YOU KNOW?

New Yorker Elijah Pratt patented the first rubber nipple in 1845,
but it didn't receive rave reviews. The India rubber material used
in its production had an unusual taste, and no matter how hungry they were, babies weren't all that thrilled with the rubber
nipple. But Pratt's prototype pretty much got the ball rolling,
and newer, more user-friendly, soft varieties of nipples continued
to be invented.

Bouncy, Bouncy Baby

Olivia Poole was a mother of seven active youngsters when she got to thinking about her own childhood on Minnesota's White Earth Indian Reservation. She remembered how mothers there concocted a cloth harness attached to a tree branch for babies strong enough to sit but not yet at the walking stage. They'd place their babies into this harness to bounce. The creation gave these eager-to-get-moving babies a chance to exercise their legs, enjoy a little bit of independent fun and give mom a break in the process. Olivia and her husband Joseph took that seed of an idea and, after moving to British Columbia, Canada, in the 1950s, the couple designed and produced what we know today as the Jolly Jumper.

Baby's First Food

Drs. Theodore Drake, Frederick Tisdall and Alan Brown developed pablum in 1931 in response to what they believed were senseless infant deaths from malnutrition and illness born of poor food storage options.

These doctors, hailing from the Hospital for Sick Children in Toronto, Ontario, sold their formula for the flaky cereal to Mead Johnson. They also sold the recipe for the "Sunwheat biscuit"—a great treat for toddlers that could also be dissolved with water and served as a nutritious cereal option to infants. Royalties for the formula were donated back to the Hospital for Sick Children Pediatric Research Foundation.

DID YOU  KNOW?

The name pablum comes from the Latin word *pabulum* (pab-you-lum), meaning "foodstuff."

KEEPING BABY DRY

Just how to best deal with your newborn's need to get rid of
bodily waste is an age-old problem that has witnessed
the invention of countless ingenious products. In the
earliest days of the "civilized world," as we'll refer to it,
everything from large leaves to animal skins and, yes,
moss (the dried variety, I hope) were used to swathe baby's
bottom. One source explained that some cultures wrapped
babies in "swaddling bands," or strips of cloth were used to
bundle baby into a neat, controllable little package.
The idea sounds more than just a little constricting and
leaves you wondering how the material kept baby dry.

The Obvious Choice

The advent of cloth diapers as we know them today didn't come about until the late 1890s. That's when an American-based company started mass-producing the product. The problem was that the cloth and the tradition of "swaddling" babies, as you can imagine, greatly restricted the flow of fresh air on the baby's tender skin. Couple that with the high acidity of urine, and it's a no-brainer that skin problems erupted—quite literally.

A New Era in Butt Care

By the 1950s, a bright and inventive Indiana housewife named Marion Donovan started thinking that there had to be a better way to deal with her baby's wet diapers. By then, rubber panties that were placed over cloth diapers were on the market, but their design wasn't all that effective. Marion had more than a few ideas on how to improve on the product. She ripped down her shower curtain and sewed it into a more effective rubber liner, complete with a safety snap that replaced the need for a sharp pin. The "Boater," as she called it, worked so well with her youngster that she attempted to market the product. When it was clear she wasn't being overwhelmed with offers from enthusiastic manufacturers, she decided to produce and market the Boater on her own. The Boater hit store shelves in 1949 and was an immediate hit among housewives everywhere for whom washing linens and baby clothes soiled by leaky diapers, not to mention the diapers themselves, took a good chunk of joy out of being a new mom. Donovan acquired a patent for the Boater, which she sold in 1951 to the Keko Corporation.

The Disposable Option

Marion Donovan's inventive mind didn't rest with the creation of a better cloth diapering system. She had no sooner perfected the Boater when the idea of creating a waterproof, disposable diaper started whirling around in that brilliant mind of hers.

For this project she had to develop a type of paper that was strong enough to handle the job while at the same time absorbent enough to protect baby's bottom. Once she perfected her idea, would you be surprised to learn that once again, she couldn't find a company interested in buying it? According to the American-based Famous Women Inventors website, manufacturers considered her idea "superfluous and impractical." It wasn't until 1961 that Victor Mills decided Donovan's idea did indeed have some merit, and that, my friends, is how Pampers came to be!

Diaper Dilemma

Depending on what type of diapers you're planning to use, you will need to change a newborn's soggy bottom every hour, except when you're having one of those rare naps your new baby allows you. Of course, if you're a new parent pondering whether you should use what some call the "environmentally friendly" option of cloth diapers or the "sanity-sustaining" disposable kind, you might want to have a look at some of the following statistics collected on the issue just to help confuse you a little more:

☛ During a newborn's first month, expect to change diapers at least 12 to 16 times per day. If you use disposable diapers, and depending on the brand you choose, this will likely lighten your wallet by about $72 per month.

☛ Most parents going the cloth diaper route buy about 36 diapers, which means you'll replace taking your aromatic garbage out several times a day with doing additional laundry at least every second day.

☛ Like disposables, different sizes of cloth diapers are required for babies as they grow. This means that although you've spend a whack of cash buying your newborn the new and improved cloth diapers available on the market, by the time your baby is six months old, you'll need another, larger set.

Chances are, unless you have a small youngster who, unlike most, isn't growing like a bad weed, you'll need to buy a larger size again at least one or two times until that apple of your eye is potty trained.

☞ In case you were already wondering just when potty training takes place, don't hold your breath. Most toddlers aren't toilet trained until they're between two and three years of age so you have a while to go yet!

☞ Speaking of potty training, some health-care professionals (and frustrated mothers) have speculated that it's actually harder to teach a toddler in disposable diapers than it is to teach a youngster wearing cloth. The reason for this is quite simple—a wet cloth diaper feels yucky, and most youngsters prefer to stay dry. Disposables, on the other hand, are absorbent and are usually changed long before they'd ever feel wet.

☞ Sources conflict on the exact number, but a conservative estimate suggests a child will have at least 5000 (and, for the extremely diligent parent, as many as 11,000) diaper changes before being potty trained.

☞ If the above figures are even remotely correct, and if you're one of the many parents going the disposable diaper route, that means you've helped contribute to the roughly 27 billion butt huggers (or more than 3.5 million tons of garbage) dumped in U.S. landfills in any single year.

☞ If that sort of thing gives you the environmental shivers, but your lifestyle is such that setting aside the extra time required to wash your own cloth diapers isn't possible, why not consider a diaper service? Although it's unclear exactly when the first diaper service set up shop, the idea became quite popular in the early 1900s and remains a viable option for folks looking to go the cloth route. A diaper service delivers the size of diapers you need throughout the week and picks up and cleans soiled diapers.

☞ Some folks argue that there is an environmental impact when using cloth diapers—the use of electricity and water, for example. Environment Canada is one national agency that's very much on the side of cloth. As one website states, "cloth diapers have already been recognized by Environmental Choice (Environment Canada) as offering environmental advantages when compared with 'disposable' diapers. Using diaper services makes them even better."

Toss of the Coin

Whether you decide to go cloth or disposable, here are a few other opinions on the pros and cons to both options:

☞ In 2001, Ohio State University published an article outlining the pros and cons of disposable versus cloth diapers. They stated "neither diaper type is clearly superior in all areas."

☞ The Ohio paper highlights a 1990 study by the Energy and Environmental Profile Analysis of Children's Disposable and Cloth Diapers. It suggests that "cloth diapers used twice as much energy and four times as much water as disposables, and created greater air and water pollution than disposables."

☞ There is no clear, objective indicator that babies are more prone to getting diaper rash from cloth or disposable diapers. One source suggests that disposable diapers are more absorbent and pull moisture away from your baby's skin, hence preventing diaper rash, while another states that cloth diapers are changed more frequently, which helps avoid diaper rash.

☞ It is estimated that it can take anywhere between 250 and 500 years for a disposable diaper to decompose.

☞ A cloth diaper can be used between 50 and 200 times. After that, you can retire it to the rag bucket.

DID YOU KNOW?

In 1979, Oregon was the first state in the U.S. to consider banning the sale of disposable diapers. Although it introduced several incentives to using diaper services, it was Nebraska that first issued a ban. In 1989, the state legislature issued a ban on the sale of non-biodegradable diapers. The law went into effect in 1993.

The Bottom Line

Whether you choose cloth or disposable diapers, you have to scoop the poop somehow—and there's no definitive answer as to the best way of doing that! And if all this is about as clear as mud, and you're really confused as to what option to go with, consider the cloth versus disposable issue a primer on being a parent!

Toilet Training

Toddlers are usually ready to begin the toilet training process somewhere between 24 and 27 months old. (Remember, this is only an average, and lots of kids fall on either side of that average.) There are a number of signs that might suggest your child is ready for that first great step toward independence (and the conclusion of your cloth versus disposable diaper dilemma). However, one of the clearest signs that you might be getting there is if your youngster takes a nap and wakes up dry. That's the time to head to the potty and praise the life out of your child!

TWINS

Twins are usually quite proud that they are one of a pair, and they make their twinhood known. Still, there are a few famous folks who, when you learn they were twins, might surprise you!

Historic Twins

The Old Testament's Jacob and Esau were the Bible's famous twosome. Sadly, there was more than just a little sibling rivalry between them. Esau, the firstborn, was supposed to inherit his father's considerable fortune. While out hunting one day, hungry and near death, he came upon Jacob, who was cooking lentil soup over an open fire. Esau asked his brother for some food, but Jacob would only comply if Esau gave him his birthright. The agreement was reinforced later that day when Jacob fooled his father into thinking he was Esau. Jacob received the paternal blessing, which led to an ongoing feud between the descendants of the two brothers. Jacob later fathered the 12 tribes of Israel.

The Two Rs

Although there were others, Romulus and Remus were perhaps one of the most famous sets of twins in Roman mythology—and with a mother like priestess Rhea Silvia and a father known as the "god of war," or Mars, it's no wonder. Greek historian Mestrius Plutarchus wrote that Romulus was the founder and first king of Rome, but that didn't happen without dispute and tragedy. Romulus and his brother argued over which of them the gods favored. To settle the disagreement, the brothers stood on opposite hills, waiting for a sign from the heavens. The sign came in the form of a flock of birds circling above Romulus. Romulus took this as confirmation of his authority and set about establishing Rome. Remus was none too pleased, and after one particularly loud argument, Romulus killed his brother.

Rare Finds

Another famous set of television twins can be found on the set of the *Antiques Roadshow*. Furniture appraisers Leigh and Leslie Keno have been breaking good, and sometimes not so good, news to antique collectors on the PBS series since 1997. Leigh and Leslie were born in Herkimer County, New York, on March 14, 1957, and are identical twins.

T 'n' T

Anyone familiar with the sitcom *Sister, Sister*, which ran from 1994 to 1999, are likely familiar with Tia and Tamera Mowry. The identical twins, born in Gelnhausen, Germany, on July 6, 1978, refocused their attention on their studies after the series was canceled. However, they never entirely left the entertainment industry, and both have aspirations of continuing their acting careers.

Big and Little Screen

Identical twins Jeremy and Jason London were born on November 7, 1972. Jeremy was a regular on the television series *Party of Five* and *7th Heaven*, while Jason is more committed to the big screen. You can see his most recent work in the Warner Brothers picture *Grind*.

Two Vins?

Vin Diesel's acting credits are well known to his fans, but the fact that he has a twin brother might be a lesser-known bit of trivia. Mark Vincent (Vin's real name) and his brother Paul were born on July 18, 1967. Paul isn't an actor but is involved in the entertainment industry, working as a film editor.

'70s Show Surprise

Ashton Kutcher's list of credits include a professional modeling career prior to landing a job as the character Michael Kelso on the sitcom *That '70s Show*. He also created the MTV show *Punk'd* and has several movie credits. Ashton was born on February 7, 1978, and has a fraternal twin named Michael.

Sad Loss

Pop icon Justin Timberlake was born on January 31, 1981, and entered this world as one part of a set of twins. Justin's sister, Laura Katherine, died shortly after birth.

Two for One

Fast-forward to present-day Hollywood. and you'll find a few prolific twins hanging about in studios here and there. Perhaps the most renowned is a set of twins who made their debut as babes in the television sitcom *Full House*. Of course, initially the audience wasn't aware that baby Michelle Tanner was actually being played by two babies. The show's producers helped disguise the fact by listing their television credits as "Mary-Kate

Ashley Olsen." But it wasn't long before Mary-Kate and Ashley Olsen gained increasing notoriety, and the viewing public fell in love with both of them. As they grew, the twins started playing themselves in such movies as *To Grandmother's House We Go* and *It Takes Two*, and today they've branched out into their own fashion line of clothing. The Olsen twins were born in Sherman Oaks, California, on June 13, 1986.

The King's Surprise

Rock 'n' roll's king supreme, Elvis Aaron Presley, was born on January 8, 1935. He, too, was born a twin. Brother Jesse Garon Presley was stillborn.

British Elite

Jane Seymour is another Hollywood icon with an impressive list of credits, and although she doesn't have a twin sibling, she is the mother of twins. Sons Johnny and Kris were born in 1995.

No Longer Desperate

Marcia Cross of *Desperate Housewives* fame birthed fraternal twin girls in 2007. Cross was 44 when she and stockbroker hubby Tom Mahoney welcomed Savannah and Eden into the world on February 20.

Double It Up

Actress Julia Roberts gave birth to fraternal twins, a daughter named Hazel and son Phinnaeus, on November 28, 2004. In 2006, the celebrity magazine *Star* reported Julia and hubby Danny Moder were once again going through fertility treatments and hoping for another "boy-and-girl pair to round out the household."

DID YOU KNOW?

On February 22, 2008, Jennifer Lopez and husband Marc Anthony welcomed baby Max and Emme into their busy lives.

Twice Is Nice

The country music sensation, the Dixie Chicks, is composed of three female members, two of whom have birthed twins. Martie Maguire said hello to her set of fraternal twins Eva Ruth and Kathleen "Katie" Emilie on April 27, 2004, and almost a year later, Emily Robinson welcomed her fraternal twins Julianna Tex and Henry Benjamin on April 14, 2005.

Twins Again?

Loretta Lynn and husband Oliver, also known as "Mooney" or "Doolittle" ("Doo" for short), married shortly after Loretta celebrated her 14th birthday. By the time she was 18, the couple had already had four children, so when Loretta delivered twin daughters, Patsy and Peggy, in 1964, her family really blossomed! You can't help but wonder if this happy event formed part of the lyrics of her 1972 hit, "One's on the Way."

Foxy Duo

Canadian-born actor Michael J. Fox and his equally talented wife Tracy Pollan welcomed identical twin daughters Aquinnah Kathleen and Schuyler Frances into their family in 1996.

Writing Twins

When it comes to getting advice on anything from hangnails to a troubled marriage, North Americans spent nearly five decades reading the wise words of "Ann Landers" or "Dear Abby." But most avid fans likely weren't aware that the two women weren't only friends and rivals, they were also identical twins. Esther Pauline Friedman (Ann Landers) and Pauline Esther Friedman (Dear Abby) were born on July 4, 1918. Initially, the sisters were quite close, so close that when they planned their weddings in 1939, they decided to hold a joint ceremony. However, after they both started their careers as advice columnists in the 1950s, competition eventually led to a severed relationship that, some sources suggest, wasn't ever completely reconciled when Ann Landers died in 2002.

Flights of Fantasy

Twins don't always mean double the joy and double the enthusiasm; sometimes they mean double the brilliance. That's certainly the case for British-born twins Suresh and Jyoti Guptara. These enterprising and imaginative youngsters became bestselling writers when Tara Press released their novel *Conspiracy of Calaspia* in November 2006, the first installment of the fantasy series *Insanity Saga*. The twins were only 11 years old when they completed their first draft, and were 17 when *Conspiracy of Calaspia* hit the bestseller list.

Wordsmith Extraordinaire
While these twins weren't writers in their own right, their father is considered by most literary scholars as the greatest writer of all time. Shakespeare and wife Anne Hathaway baptized their twins, a baby boy named Hamnet and his sister Judith, at Holy Trinity Church on February 2, 1585.

Fictional Twins

Nan and Bert and their younger twin siblings, Flossie and Freddie, of *The Bobbsey Twins* fame, are perhaps the most famous fictional twins of the last 100 years. Edward Stratemeyer penned the series, which contained a phenomenal 72 books, under the ghost name, Laura Lee Hope. The first book hit store shelves in 1904, making it the twins' official birth year.

The Weasley Duo
If book sales are any indication—and in the United States alone, an estimated 90 million copies of J.K. Rowlings *Harry Potter* series of books have been sold—Fred and George Weasley must certainly rival the Bobbsey twins as the most famous twins of juvenile literature.

Lost, Then Found
A young Hayley Mills played a dual role in the 1961 Disney film *The Parent Trap*. In this movie, the two female characters (both played by Mills) meet at a summer camp and uncover a few family secrets, not the least of which is that they're identical twins. If you want to know more, you'll just have to rent the movie!

Longest-Living Twins

Sarah and Ellen Hall may not have been all that unusual for a large part of their life as twins, but they've recently hit the record books in a big way. As of this writing, the women—born on May 29, 1902—had celebrated their 106th birthday. The sisters are not only credited with being the longest-living set of twins born in Canada but are also the longest-living twins in the world—and the *Guinness Book of Records* agrees. According to one news report near the sisters' 105th birthday, they say they owe their long and happy life to "clean living."

The Love of a Grandma

One of the more unique twin stories is that of Rosinete Serrao. The 51-year-old Brazilian woman made interesting fertility history when she gave birth to her own twin grandsons. The bouncing baby boys were born on September 28, 2007. Rosinete agreed to act as a surrogate mother for her 27-year-old daughter Claudia. The young woman and her husband were unable to conceive, but Claudia's eggs and her husband's sperm were used in the successful artificial insemination process.

Political Twins

George W. Bush is more than just the 43rd president of the United States of America, he's also the father of twin girls. Fraternal twins Barbara and Jenna were born on November 25, 1981. Because of their parents' positions in the White House, the girls are often referred to as the "First Twins."

DID YOU KNOW?

One of the more famous twins, at least for racing fans, are race-car drivers Mario and Aldo Andretti, who were born on February 28, 1940, in what was then known as Montona d'Istria, Italy.

Pitching Pair

Major league baseball lays claim to left-handed pitchers Mark and Mitch Mimbs. The brothers are listed by one source as "the first identical twins to pitch against each other in a major league baseball game."

The World of Hockey

NHL hockey stars Henrik and Daniel Sedin were born in Omskoldsvik, Sweden, on September 26, 1980, and have played hockey together since they were youngsters. As luck would have it, the identical twins were good enough—and committed sufficiently to each other—to play on the same team in the Swedish Elite League during the 1997–98 season. Surprisingly, they continued to play together in the NHL, landing second and third draft picks with the Vancouver Canucks in the 1999 NHL Entry Draft.

Famous Family

Offensive powerhouses Ron and Rich Sutter are another set of famous NHL twins. Born on December 2, 1963 in Viking, Alberta, the pair was the youngest of six brothers who made up the Sutter hockey dynasty.

Hold Them High

Women have only started making a name for themselves in the boxing ring, and California-born twins Dora and Cora Webber have certainly had a hand in that process. The sisters, born in 1958, started out their career in 1979, and to date are the only twin women boxing in a professional capacity.

Double Trouble

When identical twins are separated at birth, oftentimes they go on to live similar lives. Some researchers suggest this finding reinforces the belief that identical twins share more than just their DNA—and if a look at the criminal justice system is any indication, chances are that if one twin is a bad apple, the other might be as well. According to a report published in May 2003, 80 sets of identical twins were incarcerated in Virginia prisons.

Criminal Twins

In January 1913, after being arrested 150 times and having peace officers doing a double take on each occasion, Ebenezer Albert Fox and Albert Ebenezer Fox eventually found themselves behind bars. The identical twin brothers were born in Symonds Green, Stevenage, Hertfordshire, England, in 1857, to a solid middle-class couple, but they started to dodge the law from an early age. The two worked together, illegally poaching for a living and providing alibis for one another. Their criminal antics were partly responsible for the development of fingerprint analysis.

Sibling Rivalry

The very sad story of identical twins Jenna and Sunny Han makes ancient legends like those of Romulus and Remus so much more real. The identical twin girls were born in South Korea in April 1974. After a series of unfortunate family issues, Jenna was tried and found guilty for conspiracy to murder Sunny. Jenna won't be eligible for parole until 2020.

Rocking London

Organized crime in Britain boasted a set of identical twin king-pins. Ronald and Reginald Kray were born on October 24, 1933. Together they reigned supreme in London's East End during the 1950s and 1960s.

Identical Struggles

June and Jennifer Gibbons were born in Barbados on April 11, 1963. These identical twins struggled with a speech impediment, and because of their West Indian heritage, faced considerable racism at school. After years of turmoil, the sisters turned to petty crime, resulting in them being committed to the Broadmoor Hospital for the criminally insane, in Berkshire, England. Jennifer died in 1993, and to this day the cause of her death isn't clear. Before her death, the sisters made a pact that if one of them should pass away, the other should try to live a normal life. In many respects, June has tried to do that, even taking up residence with her partner in 2005.

Identical Experiences

They say identical twins are so close they sometimes know what the other is thinking or can feel the other's pain. In the case of identical twins Nicole Cramer and Naomi Sale of Auburn, Indiana, the belief appears to be true—at least with the young women and their baby boys. Both Nicole and Naomi gave birth at the same hospital on January 23, 2007. Dr. Thaddeus Weghorst delivered a baby boy for each woman. Naomi had been scheduled for a cesarean, and Dr. Weghorst couldn't help but wonder, after delivering her baby, if he'd be back for sister Nicole later that same day. Sure enough, shortly after visiting Naomi and her baby Ethan, Nicole went into labor. Ninety minutes later she delivered her son, Carter. As you now know from reading this book that it's the father's sperm that decides the sex of the baby, the unique twin bond isn't the reason the sisters both had a boy. But it does make for a nice coincidence to add to the story, don't you think?

DID YOU KNOW?

Sparrow Hospital in Lansing, Michigan, like many other hospitals, is used to delivering babies. But on June 30, 2006, the skill and energy of the entire maternity ward staff was taxed to the max. That's because in the span of 32 hours, they delivered not one, not two, not even three sets of twins. That day, staff assisted in six twin deliveries!

Twins or Triplets?

Identical sisters Ruby and Tilly Kersey are unique in their own right. But their story is more interesting than your typical identical twin story. You see, the sisters have another sibling—Gracie. All three sisters shared the same birth mother and came into the world on the same September day in 2006. What they didn't share was a womb. It appears their mother, Hannah, had two wombs. Although the British mother knew of her condition, which in clinical terms is called uterus didelphys, doctors advised her that it would be unlikely for her to conceive in both wombs. Of course, she proved the odds wrong. The three babies were born by cesarean seven weeks before their due date.

DID YOU KNOW?

There are cases on record in which a woman with uterus didelphys has conceived and carried a single baby in each womb at the same time, but the Kersey's triplet birth is the first story of its kind.

Making the Record Book

Lauren Cohen of Paramus, New Jersey, made American history in 2006 when she gave birth to twins, a boy and a girl, at New York Presbyterian Hospital. Cohen, already a mother of a two-year-old, was 59 at the time of the twins' birth, making her the oldest woman to give birth to twins in the U.S. With a spouse 20 years her junior, Cohen isn't concerned for her children's future. She knows they'll always be in good hands!

A year later, Frieda Birnbaum edged Cohen out of that record-holding position when she welcomed twin boys in May 2007. Birnbaum was 60 when she gave birth at the Hackensack University Medical Center in Hackensack, New Jersey. After being married for 38 years, the Birnbaums already had three children—two adult children and a six-year-old—at the time of the twins' birth.

THREE OF A KIND

*If you think double means trouble, there's something to
be said about the triple threat that three of a kind can be!
Amazingly, there are a lot of triplets who have collectively
laid some claim to fame or other.*

More Amazing by the Minute

As they say, some things are just meant to be. When Angela
Magdaleno gave birth to triplets in 2002, she and her husband
Alfredo were happy with their growing family. The couple
already had two girls, and the triplets gave them the "big" family they'd always wanted. Angela had undergone in vitro fertilization with her triplets, and because the couple wasn't planning
on any more children, Angela was using birth control. So when
her doctor told her she was pregnant, she was surprised. When
she was also told she was carrying quadruplets, she was overwhelmed. On July 6, 2006, the Magdalenos welcomed two boys
and two girls into their already substantial family of five children. And just to add a little twist to the scenario, doctors suspect that the boys, who were born second and third, are
identical twins.

Medical Intervention
The world's first-ever test-tube triplets were Aaron, Jessica and
Chenara Guare, born on June 8, 1983, in Adelaide, Australia.

Chinese Challenge
China's first set of test-tube triplets was born in Shanghai on
November 6, 1999, 10 years after China's first test-tube baby
made its appearance. The triplets, two girls and a boy, were born
at the Shanghai Medical Sciences University hospital, but their
names were not released.

DID YOU KNOW?

Just a month later, on December 20, 1999, a family in Shenyang, a city in northeast China, delivered the first test-tube triplets that part of the country had ever seen. In this case, two boys and a girl made their grand entry at a hospital connected with Chinese Medical Sciences University.

Triple Take

Although triplets are not that common, at least one set made a name for themselves in the same industry. Nicole, Erica and Jaclyn Dahm, a set of identical triplets born on December 12, 1977, made headlines in the December 1998 issue of *Playboy*. The three blonde-haired sisters were all featured Playmates in that month's issue of the magazine. The young women have also starred in numerous films, made-for-TV movies and serials.

Three Hit the Screen

On a tamer note, Leanna, Monica and Joy Creel, a triple threat born on August 27, 1970, hit the television world at a young age. The triplets starred in two Disney movies, *Parent Trap 3* and *Parent Trap 4: Hawaiian Honeymoon*. Leanna and Monica also acted on an episode of *Beverly Hills, 90210*.

Animation Creation

Donald Duck might not have had a hard time getting into trouble all by himself, but do you remember the chaos when his three nephews came to visit? Huey, Dewey and Louis Duck, the fictional creation of Disney artists Ted Osborne and Al Taliaferro, were Donald's mischievous nephews, and because their first appearance on-screen was on April 15, 1938, I guess you could call that their official birthday!

Classy Trio

Edith, Elena and Milly Boyd, known by their professional name as the Del Rubio Triplets, were born in Panama on August 23, 1921. The story goes that they had stars in their eyes from an early age and were determined to make it to Hollywood, which they did. They worked primarily as a lounge act in the 1950s and 1960s, but in the 1980s they ventured into TV land, appearing on the shows *Married with Children*, *Full House* and *The Golden Girls*. According to one report, the sisters were the oldest living triplets until 1996, when Edith died of colon cancer at the age of 75. Elena passed away on March 19, 2001, at the age of 79. Milly is the only surviving sister as of this writing.

OTHER FAMOUS MULTIPLES

Once you get into the four or more single birth categories, especially if they're all identical, you're famous no matter what you do for a living. According to some sources, there have been cases in which women have carried as many as 15 fetuses during a single pregnancy. Of course, it's impossible for one woman to carry that many fetuses to full term, but the story is amazing nonetheless.

Four Is, Well, More!

According to one source, the first same-sex set of quadruplets to all live to adulthood were Roberta, Mary, Mona and Leota Keys. The girls were born on June 4, 1915, in Hollis, Oklahoma, and all graduated from Baylor University in 1937.

Four and Identical

As mentioned earlier, the chances of having identical quadruplets are extremely small, so whenever there's an instance of such a claim, it makes the news. On October 24, 1974, the Hansen family of San Antonio, Texas, was propelled into the public spotlight when Alison, Brooke, Claire and Darcy were born.

A Canadian First

Canada's first set of identical quadruplets was Carrie Dawn, Jennie Lee, Mary Beth and Patty Ann, born on December 17, 1982, in Calgary, Alberta. The rare event was amazingly duplicated in the same city when Karen and J.P. Jepp welcomed Autumn, Brooke, Calissa and Dahlia into the world on August 12, 2007. That both of Canada's identical quads were born in Calgary makes the odds even more unbelievable.

Five, and Alive

Probably the world's most famous quintuplets are the Dionne sisters. Born in Corbeil, Ontario, on May 28, 1934, to Elzire and Olivia Dionne, the five identical sisters made their grand entry two months shy of a full nine-month pregnancy. The early birth complicated their situation. Annette, Cecile, Emilie, Marie and Yvonne had a combined birth weight of 13.6 pounds, which made their future precarious, indeed. Because they needed extensive medical care, and their parents weren't in the financial position to provide them with the care they needed, the Ontario government took custody of the girls.

Over time, the quints grew stronger and even thrived, surprising just about everyone involved in their care. Sadly, as they grew and word spread of the five little darlings, people wanted to see the babies, and for the first several years of the sisters' lives, they were exhibited three times a day. People paraded past their toy room at the "Quintland" residence and viewed the girls through a one-way screen as they played. It's been estimated that these thrice-daily exhibits raised about a half a billion dollars for the government providing their care. The girls survived into adulthood—prior to their birth, there were no records of newborn quintuplets surviving longer than a few days.

World's First Sextuplets
The family of Barry and Sheila Thorns ballooned immensely when Sheila gave birth to the world's first set of sextuplets born alive (at least according to modern medical records) in Birmingham, England, on October 2, 1968. Sadly, three of the six babies died within the first two weeks.

The Rosenkowitz Six
Cape Town, South Africa, is the birth home of Grant, David, Jason, Liz, Nicky and Emma, more commonly known as the Rosenkowitz sextuplets. The siblings, born on January 11, 1974, have the distinction of being the first sextuplets in the world to survive. By 2004, all but one had immigrated to the United Kingdom. Only Grant, an exercise specialist by profession, continued to make his home in Cape Town.

A Birthing Miracle
It wasn't until 1980 that the United Kingdom recorded its first set of surviving sextuplets. Hannah, Lucy, Ruth, Sarah, Kate and Jenny Walton were born on November 18, 1983, and along with being a birthing miracle for their parents—who, after 12 failed fertility treatments, had been told they couldn't have children—the girls also had the distinction of being the "world's first all-female surviving sextuplets." Looks like the number 13 was a charm for the Waltons!

Known by Their Offspring
Thomas and Edith Bonham of Wiltshire, England, are on record as having the first recorded set of septuplets born.

The couple, who lived in the 1400s, was said to have birthed seven children from a single pregnancy. Their story was so widely known and publicized at the time that they became known as the parents of "the seven children at one birth," and the couple's stone effigies can still be found at the Church of St. Giles at Great Wishford in Wiltshire. It isn't clear if all seven survived the birth, but it is highly unlikely.

There Were Seven in the Bed
The award for the first set of surviving septuplets in the world goes to the McCaughey family of Des Moines, Iowa. The four boys and three girls were born on November 19, 1997, at just 31 weeks' gestation and weighed between 2 pounds, 5 ounces and 3 pounds, 4 ounces. Within a year of their birth, fans of the family could purchase McCaughey septuplet dolls—that's one inventive way to pay for all the nappies they needed.

Another Seven
Hasna and Mohammed Humair weren't at all prepared to hit the spotlight with the force they did on January 14, 1998. The couple, who lived in Abha, Saudi Arabia, was expecting quadruplets but ended up with seven babies that day. All seven survived, making them the second set of septuplets in the world to survive.

Trying for Eight?
There are at least six sets of octuplets on record:

☛ The first set, with four of each sex, was born on March 10, 1967, to Maria Teresa Lopez de Sepulveda of Mexico City, Mexico. Sadly, all eight babies died.

☛ An unidentified 25-year-old Turkish woman birthed octuplets in 1985. All eight babies died within three days of their birth.

☞ In August 1996, 32-year-old Mandy Alwood tried to save all eight of her babies rather than accept medical advice to abort some of the unborn fetuses. Her valiant efforts failed.

☞ In December of that same year, a 31-year-old Spanish woman named Rosario Clavijo carried eight fetuses to term, but only six survived birth.

☞ Mariella Mazzara and Giovanni Pierrera of Trapani, Sicily, were also hoping all eight of their babies would make it outside the womb when Mariella delivered at just 25 weeks gestation on September 13, 2000. Seven of the babies, four boys and three girls, were live births, and within a month, three of those babies had died. It's unclear if the remaining four survived infancy.

☞ The first set of octuplets born in the U.S. made their grand entry in Houston, Texas. They were born to the Chukwu family in December 1998. Baby Odera died shortly after birth, and the remaining seven siblings—sisters Ebuka, Chidi, Echerem, Gorom, Chima, and brothers Ikem and Jioke—made their first public appearance just before their first birthday.

Holy Mother of Eight!

The Kaiser Permanente Bellflower Medical Center in California made history when doctors there delivered octuplets on January 26, 2009. The six boys and two girls made their grand entry into the world at 30 weeks gestation and weighed in between 1 pound 8 ounces and 3 pounds 4 ounces. By the time their story hit the news media all eight were said to be in stable condition. Even the smallest, a "feisty" boy, one of two babies who needed the help of a breathing tube, had the device removed. Although the babies will remain in hospital for about two months, and face numerous challenges ahead, as of press time all eight babies were breathing independently.

Until the birth, doctors were only expecting seven babies—the eighth bundle of joy was a surprise to everyone. The miracle birth is the second case of live octuplets to be born in the U.S., and if all goes as planned, the survival of all eight will be a historic world first.

Fragile at Nine

Three reports of women carrying nonuplets are on record. The first set was born on June 13, 1971, in Sydney, Australia, but of the seven born alive, none survived. All nine of Aurina Mat Saad's babies were born alive on March 26, 1999, in Malaysia, but they died, and the strongest only survived for six hours. Another case of a Sudanese woman carrying nonuplets in 2002 is unconfirmed.

Tough Choices

As is most often the case, multiple pregnancies are often the result of fertility treatments, and when women are expecting extraordinarily large number of babies, it's not uncommon for doctors to abort some of the fetuses. Such was the case of 23-year-old Zoe Efstathiou of Cyprus in 1996. Zoe and her husband, 27-year-old Demetris, already had a baby girl in 1994 with the help of fertility treatments and wanted another child. What they ended up with was a multiple pregnancy that hit the record books.

After several tests during Zoe's first trimester, they couple thought they were expecting six babies, but after a few more tests, an amazing 11 heartbeats were detected. Because even in the most exceptional case a woman's body will likely reject 11 fetuses, after extensive consultation with gynecologist Andreas Patsalides and other health professionals at the Makarios Hospital in Nicosia, seven fetuses were removed. Further information on the final result of that pregnancy isn't publicly known.

Multiple Multiples

Italian Renaissance philosopher Giovanni Pico della Mirandola (1463–94) recorded the story of an Italian woman who gave birth to 11 babies back in the 1400s. Making this story even more unbelievable is that the woman, known only as Dorothea, was rumored to have given birth to nine babies after an earlier pregnancy.

DID YOU KNOW?

Odd as Dorothea's story may be, she isn't the only woman in history to have a large multiple pregnancy without the use of fertility drugs. Twenty-four-year-old Sciortino de Allavatti miscarried 12 fetuses in 1992. Allavatti did *not* use fertility drugs, propelling her into the record books as the woman to naturally conceive the highest number of multiples.

Top of the Line

The largest number of fetuses recorded in a woman during a single pregnancy took place in 1971. Dr. Gennaro Montanino removed an amazing 15 fetuses of four-month gestation from a 35-year-old woman in Italy on July 22, 1971. This multiple pregnancy was the result of fertility treatments.

Love and Tragedy

When Diane Blood married her sweetheart, Stephen, she dreamed of the day they'd welcome their first child into the world. So when her husband died in 1995 from bacterial meningitis, that dream seemed impossible. Unless, of course, she harvested his sperm—a procedure completed just before he died. The action caused all kinds of backlash from agencies arguing the ethics of the action to the legal wing of the British government. The focal point of the argument was that the decision to harvest Stephen's sperm was apparently a private and verbal discussion between husband and wife, and the sperm were harvested at a time when he was unable to provide his consent.

Diane had to go to court to obtain permission to use the sperm and to obtain the fertility treatments necessary for her to conceive. She was denied the right to fertility treatments in the United Kingdom; the government, citing the Human Fertilisation and Embryology Act of 1990, required "written consent of a donor to the taking of his sperm."

Initially, permission to undergo the procedure was denied absolutely, but a Court of Appeal decision allowed the woman to travel to Belgium for the procedure. It wasn't until the year 2000 that the couple's son Liam was born. Thrilled though she was, Diane was also determined to provide her son with a sibling—and in 2002, baby Joel was born.

Diane's battle wasn't over yet. The law required the boy's father be listed as "unknown" or a blank space left where birth documents require the father's name be entered, something that quite obviously appalled Diane. She continued to fight her cause all the way up to the House of Lords, and in September 2003, she celebrated a victory that resulted in changes to existing laws. It is now legal for children conceived after their father's death to have the father officially recognized on the child's birth certificate. And if you think Diane's case is unique, think again. At the time this bill was passed, an estimated 50 families with children conceived and born under the same circumstances were expected to benefit from the decision.

DID YOU KNOW?

Ohio's famous annual "Twins Days" festival appropriately takes place in Twinsburg the first weekend of August. It's billed as the "largest gathering of twins and multiples in the world," with its inaugural event held in 1976.

STRUGGLING THROUGH TOUGH TIMES

While the vast majority of babies are born perfect, with all their fingers and toes, some babies do face unique challenges. When I delivered my fourth child in 1987, everything looked normal enough. Aside from aspirating a little bit of amniotic fluid during his birth, Nathan was given a clean bill of health. But he had a raspy way of breathing that, despite my pediatrician's reassurance that it was the result of dry air or a stubborn case of croup, worried me.

I was right to worry. Just an hour or so after I'd put Nathan to bed one night, I went to check on him. As a chronic worrier, I had a habit of placing my hand on his back to make sure he was breathing. His body was still. Panic-stricken, I yanked him out of bed and, on noticing he was a pasty yellow color and his lips were blue, started shaking him and screaming. I'm quite certain that most of Nathan's teenage rebellion was linked to that moment of sheer terror and my panicked shaking. It took a while, but he started breathing again, and I rushed him to the hospital.

After undergoing many tests, and my continued nagging at doctors that something was definitely wrong with my son—after all, a mother of four children just knows these things—Nathan was diagnosed with a heart defect known as a double aortic arch, a type of vascular ring. The main artery from his heart had divided in two, wrapped itself around the esophagus and trachea, and joined up again.

This birth defect is considered rare, and some people can live with the condition and never know it. But for Nathan, the compression caused by the tightly wound artery was basically choking him to death. He needed surgery.

It was touch and go for some time, but Nathan had his operation and bounced back. Of course, we don't live in a perfect world, and not every medical challenge results in such a positive ending. This section is dedicated to those children who are born with a vast array of difficulties. Some of these children have survived while others have sadly passed away. But in every case, their stories, and their spirits, live on.

The Big Picture

One in every 33 babies born in the United States suffers from a birth defect. That amounts to roughly 120,000 babies born with some type of special need. Some defects, such as fetal alcohol syndrome, account for as many as five percent of the birth population, or 6000 affected babies per year, and are the result of some form of environmental exposure. Therefore, these defects are almost 100 percent preventable.

About 25 percent of birth abnormalities are genetic in nature—passed on from one or both parents at conception. Just what causes the remaining 70 percent of birth defects is less clear. It's thought that most cases involve a mixture of environmental factors, behavioral practices and heredity, blended together in a unique combination.

Here are a few common birth defects that occur in the U.S. annually, according to the March of Dimes Foundation:

Birth Defect	Number of Babies
Cleft lip/palate	6800
Down syndrome	5500
Metabolic disorders	3000
Transposition of great arteries	1900
Spina bifida (open spine)	1300

Down Syndrome

According to the Mayo Clinic, "Down syndrome is the most common genetic cause of severe learning disabilities in children." In the United States, an estimated one in 700 babies is born with the genetic disorder, but as with any medical condition, not every child diagnosed with Down syndrome will experience the same difficulties. Problems with cognitive ability can range from mild to, in some cases, severe. The disorder often produces other complications as well, such as congenital heart defects, and babies with Down syndrome have unique physical characteristics, one of which is slanting eyes.

British doctor John Langdon Down first described the syndrome that would later bear his name in 1866. In 1959, French pediatrician and geneticist Jerome Lejeune further identified it as a chromosome 21 trisomy, after discovering that a Down syndrome child has three copies of the 21st chromosome instead of two.

Spina Bifida

Known by the Latin term meaning "split spine," spina bifida is a neural tube defect that occurs when the tissue surrounding the developing spinal cord doesn't close properly. In most cases, the bones in the spine are also open.

There are three types of this disorder: spina bifida occulta, spina bifida cystica and meningocele. In the first instance, the defect is hidden and often goes undiagnosed. Spina bifida occulta usually causes minimal problems, though some studies suggest people with significant back pain have later discovered they have this disorder. Spina bifida cystica is the most common and most serious of the three variations. In this case, the spinal cord might actually protrude through an opening in the spinal column. This usually prompts the need for surgery and, depending on the severity of the condition, some degree of nerve damage is quite common. Meningocele is the least common of the three varieties. The defect presents itself as a sac or cyst that contains cerebrospinal fluid. Nerve and spinal cord damage are usually present in these cases.

It's important to know that medical science has no definitive method of preventing spina bifida. However, it appears that increasing the amount of foods rich in folic acid in your diet during pregnancy can decrease chances of the fetus developing the disorder.

Medical Controversy

Being pregnant and going through labor is probably one of the toughest things a woman will ever experience. Her body is changing, she's tired and frosty at times, and morning sickness is hell. While one drug can't address all the symptoms, thalidomide, which was sold under 40 different names, was developed in 1953 to help combat morning sickness and to help pregnant women sleep. It wasn't until babies started being born with defective limbs that the public learned the drug hadn't gone through all the tests required to assess its safety. An estimated 10,000 to 12,000 babies born between 1956 and 1962 were affected. The drug was also thought to be responsible for another 8000 miscarriages. It was discovered that thalidomide wasn't safe to take during the first part of pregnancy, which is a time of rapid growth for the fetus.

In the end, the drug was taken off the market but has been found to be effective in treating some other medical conditions.

Craniopagus Parasiticus

Simply put, a baby diagnosed with craniopagus parasiticus is born with a parasitic twin head. These "second heads" are developed to various degrees, but a fetus with this condition most often dies before birth. One source suggests there have been rare instances, about 80 throughout recorded history, when the baby survived birth.

One of these babies, who over time became known as the "Two-headed Boy of Bengal," was born with an almost completely formed head attached to the top of his skull—the tops of both heads were fused together. He was born in May 1783, and the day of his birth was also the day he nearly died. The midwife attending the birth was so horrified at seeing the youngster that she threw him into the fire. Amazingly, he survived.

But his was a sad life indeed. His parents took to exhibiting him in Calcutta, and he was put away, often in a dark room and alone, between showings. In what was something of a miracle, and with no help from the medical world, the little boy seemed to be quite healthy and may have lived a long life had a cobra not bitten him at the age of four. He was buried near the city of Tumioch, but he didn't rest there long. His grave was robbed, his body mutilated, and his skull brought to England for further examination. It was discovered that each skull housed a complete and functioning brain. The skull is now housed at the Hunterian Museum of the Royal College of Surgeons of London.

Tough Surgeries

Medical scientists estimate the chances of twins being born conjoined at the head are about one in 2.5 million. Birthing a baby with a parasitic twin is even more rare. Rebeca Martinez had the distinction of being the eighth such baby in the world. Rebeca was born on December 10, 2003, in the Dominican Republic. After the initial shock of discovering that the baby was born with a parasitic head, doctors soon realized that her second head was growing faster than the other one. To give her even the slightest chance of survival, surgeons tried to remove the second head in February 2004. At first, the historic operation, involving 18 health-care professionals and lasting 11 grueling hours, appeared successful. But within a few hours, as Rebeca's body continued to try to pump blood to the parasitic head, which was now nonexistent, she began to bleed. Within seven hours after the surgery, her small, frail body couldn't handle the strain, and after suffering several heart attacks, she died.

At the age of 10 months, Manar Maged was a bit older than Rebeca when she had her surgery in February 2005. It took 13 hours for doctors at Egypt's renowned Benha Children's Hospital to remove her second head and a portion of her upper body. Not only did Manar survive the surgery, but she also lived more than one year after it. The problem was that she suffered from ongoing infections, and it was just such an infection in her brain that resulted in her death.

A Gift from God

Vinod and Susham Singh of Uttar Pradesh district in India might have worried when they first saw their darling baby girl Lali, but they considered her a gift from God nonetheless. Lali was born on March 11, 2008, and she entered this world with a defect known as craniofacial duplication. She was born with two pair of lips, two noses, two perfect pairs of eyes and two ears—all parts functioning. Photos of the baby hit media outlets around the world almost immediately after her birth, and the world couldn't help but melt when it saw her.

The Singhs, who live in the village of Saini, northeast of New Delhi, believe their daughter is the reincarnation of the Indian God Ganesha, patron of arts and sciences, and the deva of intellect and wisdom, or Durga, the Hindu goddess of valor, a fiery deity. The Singhs weren't alone in their belief. Villagers raced to see the newborn, offering gifts and money and looking for a opportunity to touch her hands or stroke her hair. As of this writing, baby Lali appears healthy and thriving.

One Head, Two Bodies

It's called ischiopagus conjoined twins, and simply put, it means a baby is born with the headless body of her twin attached in some way. Lakshmi Tatama, a little Indian girl born in 2005, was born with the lower part of the parasitic body attached to her lower body. When she was born, Lakshmi looked as if she had eight limbs, and her parents, Shambhu and Poonam, believed she was the reincarnation of the Hindu goddess of wealth, Vishnu. Unlike the goddess, who also had extra limbs, young Lakshmi went through more than 30 hours of surgery to remove the parasitic body in 2007. The surgery was made possible through Dr. Sharan Patil and a team of 30 surgeons at Sparsh Hospital in Bangalore, India. Additional surgeries have been necessary, but the young girl continues to improve, and the outlook for her future is positive.

The Face of an Angel

When Juliana Wetmore made her grand debut, her parents knew there would be some questions about her general health. Routine ultrasounds conducted in most pregnancies turned into weekly ones for Juliana's mother, but the tests only left doctors with more questions than answers. Still, this was Thom and Tami's second baby, so most of the new parent jitters had been spent on their first child. Whatever this new baby presented them with, the couple would be ready.

Juliana was born in March 2003 in Jacksonville, Florida, with Treacher Collins syndrome. The diagnosis manifested itself as an extensive craniofacial defect with as many as 40 percent of the bones in her face missing. The media, on hearing the news, labeled her the "girl who was born without a face." But no matter how devastating the reality, or how unpredictable the future, the Wetmores held firm. They never let baby Juliana feel different or less capable than her able-bodied sister. And despite Juliana's many structural problems, which have meant one surgery after another, as well as her numerous respiratory infections, the Wetmores keep life as normal as possible for their daughter. And in June 2008, they were rewarded when a proud Juliana, garbed from head to toe in cap and gown, posed for her kindergarten graduation photo. Life won't be easy for this family, but one thing is certain—it will be a rich one.

Dental Dilemma

Perfect and pink and as glorious as any newborn can be, Megan Andrews entered the world on June 29, 2007. Mom Claire Slimming was thrilled with her new daughter, but shortly after her birth it appeared baby Megan had come with a few additions. Doctors discovered Megan was born with teeth—seven, in fact. While the condition is uncommon, it's estimated that one in 2000 or 3000 babies are born with what doctors refer to as natal teeth.

The news wasn't overwhelming or strange to mom Claire, though. She had also been born with natal teeth. In Claire's case, the 12 teeth she was born with were removed when she was just a baby. Natal teeth are usually removed to prevent injuries to the tongue or swallowing a dislodged tooth—the teeth are often loose. However, because Claire has struggled with dental issues most of her life, partly as result of being born with natal teeth, she's hopeful that dental science has advanced enough to limit the difficulties baby Megan might face.

CONJOINED TWINS

Rare. There's no other word for it. The occurrences of live births of conjoined twins are so rare that babies born with this condition are immediately thrust into the spotlight. Conjoined twins are always identical. However, because of a deficiency in the twinning process sometime around the third week of gestation, the babies are born connected. There are as many as a dozen different varieties of conjoined twins. Among the rarest are craniophagus twins—twins whose heads are joined in some fashion. This happens in only two percent of conjoined cases. Dr. Joseph Warrington delivered one of the first documented cases of cephalothoracopagus monosymmetros twins in 1851. These baby girls were described as "fused at [the] head and thorax." The skeleton of these sisters is currently housed at the Mutter Museum of the College of Physicians of Philadelphia.

What follows are stories of children facing a variety of this condition. In some cases surgery to separate the children was attempted, and in others it wasn't possible to even try. In every case, these stories are amazing, and the children strong and courageous.

In the Spotlight

The conjoined twins credited for bringing this condition into the spotlight and giving it the nickname "Siamese twins" were Chang and Eng. The brothers were born in 1811 in Siam, hence the moniker Siamese twins. Legend has it that the king of Siam, King Rama II, saw the birth as a dire portent and initially ordered the twins' death. But when life continued on as usual, and no tragedy struck, the king re-examined the issue and rescinded his decree.

Stories of the brothers' lives indicate they had a happy childhood. They were able to grow and develop like other boys, and spent considerable time helping their father, who made his living as a fisherman.

The brothers didn't start exhibiting themselves until after their 16th birthday. By 1829, they'd already traveled Europe and Asia, and were bound for North America, touring with P.T. Barnum's circus. After 10 intense years of travel and putting themselves on display, the brothers were tired. They'd had enough and decided to retire from the limelight and use some of the money they'd made to buy a general store in one of the small North Carolina towns they had visited while touring. That only lasted a short while before they tried their hand at farming, took American citizenship and adopted the surname Bunker.

On April 13, 1843, Chang and Eng married the Yates sisters, Adelaide (Chang) and Sallie (Eng). Life was never easy, but it was good for a time. Both couples lived together, and all four reportedly slept in the same bed. Eng and Sallie produced 11 children through their union, and Chang and Adelaide had 10 of their own. But tension grew between brothers and sisters, and in time, the twins purchased a second house and divided their time between the sisters. With two homes and almost two dozen children to provide for, the brothers had to tour again.

As it turns out, they were quite minimally joined. Just the flesh of the abdomen, some cartilage and their livers were fused. Today, surgery to separate the two would most likely result in two healthy, separated little boys.

The brothers died in 1874, Eng just a few hours after Chang.

Italian Wonders

There's a lot of mystery surrounding Italian-born conjoined twins Giacomo and Giovanni Batista Tocci. For example, the day of their birth is known—October 4—but the year is an entirely different story. The best guess, based on the years the twins were on the exhibition circuit, places their birth year somewhere between 1875 and 1878.

The brothers were the eldest children born to Antonia Mezzano, who was 19 at the time, and they were the only children of 11 (other sources state nine) with any physical anomaly. Giacomo and Giovanni were dicephalus conjoined twins, which meant they structurally shared everything from the sixth rib down. They shared two legs, but each had two arms. Their personalities, on the other hand, couldn't be more different—one twin was an artist and an extrovert, while the other was withdrawn and temperamental. (Unfortunately, different sources credit each twin with each characteristic, so to define their personalities directly isn't possible.) Perhaps the difference in their temperaments was why the twins never learned to walk, and they primarily relied on a wheelchair for transportation.

Because humans are naturally curious, and something out of the ordinary usually gets people to open their pocketbooks, the brothers were being exhibited publicly at the disturbingly young age of one month. By the time they were young boys, they had crossed the ocean and were being shown throughout the United States. While there, they were spotted by renowned author Mark Twain and immortalized in his short story, "Those Extraordinary Twins." Also, it was believed that while they were in the U.S., they adopted the nickname "The Blended Brothers."

The latter part of their lives was just as mysterious as the twins' beginning. Once they retired from the circus, having acquired enough money to provide a comfortable living for themselves and their families, Giacomo and Giovanni disappeared from the public spotlight. Still, a few media reports have filtered through over the years. One reason for the reports may have been because members of the medical community frequently examined the twins and documented their progress.

Other reports, however, were of a more personal nature. J. Tithonus Pednaud authored an article about the brothers in *The Human Marvels* and suggested that news reports from 1904 told of how each of the brothers married. There is much dispute about the possibility. Sources also differ on the date of their death, ranging from the 1890s, shortly after they retired from their work, to 1940, which would have put them at about 63 years of age. The actual date is anyone's guess.

During their lifetime, whether it was originally their idea or not, they opened themselves to the world. Because of this, an understanding of dicephalus tetrabrachius twins began to form, and today, children born with this condition can benefit from the discoveries that followed.

Record Breakers

Russian Masha and Dasha Krivoshlyapovy were born on January 3, 1950, and died on April 17, 2003. When they died at the age of 53, they were the oldest living dicephalus conjoined twins in history.

DID YOU KNOW?

The first time a birth of conjoined twins was officially recorded was in Armenia in 945. The brothers were joined at the abdomen, and both died after attempts were made to separate them.

Taking a Chance

They were just six months shy of their 30th birthday when Ladan and Laleh Bijani agreed to undergo an operation to separate them. The young women, born on January 17, 1974, in the southwestern Iranian city of Shiraz, shared a skull, but each had her own brain. They spent their early life in an orphanage because their parents couldn't meet the girls' unique needs. Thankfully, Dr. Alireza Safaian brought them into his care, and the sisters thrived. Both studied at university and obtained law degrees. Ladan wanted to become a lawyer while her sister wanted to be a journalist—their desire for different careers was one of the reasons they wanted to be separated.

The women were aware of the risks of the surgery, one of the most severe was that they shared a vein that carried blood from their brains. As well, once doctors started operating, it was discovered their brains had fused together to some degree. From the beginning, the women knew they had a 50-50 chance of survival. But a BBC News report quoted one of the twins as saying that looking into her sister's eyes for the first time in her life was worth the risk. The twins died on July 8, 2003, within 90 minutes of each other, following their 53-hour-long separation surgery. A nation mourned their loss.

Musical Marvels

The Hungarian sisters of Szony, named Lucina and Judith, were born on October 26, 1701. What made them so unique, aside from being accomplished musicians and performing successfully throughout Europe, was that they were pygopagus twins—they were fused at the posterior and may or may not have shared a spinal cord and an anus. Lucina and Judith, who became known as the "Hungarian sisters," were just 22 when they passed away.

DID YOU KNOW?

There are more cases of conjoined sisters than conjoined brothers—about 75 percent are female and 25 percent are male.

Hollywood Bound

Also joined at the back, in this case the hips and rump, were Daisy and Violet Hilton. Born on February 5, 1908, in Brighton, East Sussex, the sisters spent their lives in the entertainment industry. Their attending physician, Dr. James Augustus Rooth, named them the first conjoined twins to be born in the United Kingdom and to survive more than a few weeks. Although they shared no major organs, they did share a circulatory system and couldn't be separated. They died on January 4, 1969, from the Hong Kong flu.

Life in the Circus

Even if they could be separated, the world's oldest set of living conjoined twins—Ronnie and Donnie Gaylon—choose not to. Born on October 28, 1951, in Dayton, Ohio, the brothers were initially protected from the entertainment world. But when their father struggled with medical bills, it became necessary to travel that route. For 36 years, the twins toured with circus sideshows in the U.S. and abroad, before retiring. When asked during a documentary produced about their lives if they would ever consider being separated, their answer was a quick and clear, "No."

Standing Firm

Lori and George (born as Dori and previously known as Reba) Schappell aren't afraid to stand up for their rights. After spending their first 24 years in an institution, having been diagnosed with an intellectual disability, adjusting to life as conjoined twins was almost a minor milestone. George took their case all the way to the governor of Pennsylvania before the diagnosis was overturned, and the young women were allowed to attend college and live on their own.

Today, George, who suffers from spina bifida and is dwarfed in comparison to her able-bodied sister Lori, maintains a career as a country music singer. She has performed across the U.S. and in Germany and Japan. The sisters have also appeared in the TV series *Nip and Tuck*. Because they share 30 percent of their brain tissue, an attempt to separate the twins would be extremely life threatening to one or both. But that's not the way they want to go anyway. Lori and George stress they're "happy as they are" and question why they should "risk our lives just to conform to what society wants." As Lori told BBC in May 2004, "My name is not 'Conjoined Twin Schappell'! My name is Lori Lynn Schappell…I am a person. I have a soul. I have a heart."

The Meaning of Teamwork

It takes teamwork and cooperation beyond belief to coordinate two lives into a conjoined body. And if you think Lori and George Schappell are a shining example of this (Lori pays to see George's concerts because she enjoys going and would attend even if they weren't conjoined), the Hensel twins are equally amazing.

When Patty and Mike Hensel were expecting their first child, they went through the typical barrage of tests every pregnant woman goes through, including an ultrasound. Everything appeared to be developing as expected. But it wasn't long after Patty arrived at the hospital to deliver in March 1990 that the doctors recognized they were dealing with an urgent situation. Patty delivered two babies, Abby and Brittany, but the identical twins shared more than just their DNA—they shared a body.

Abby and Brittany have the distinction of being one of the rarest types of conjoined twins, known as dicephalus. One source states that at birth they were given a one in 30-million chance of surviving 24 hours. They've not only survived, they've thrived.

Each girl has many of her own organs—for example, they each have a heart, stomach and gallbladder. However, they share a body in the truest sense, with two arms and two legs and a single midsection working in unison.

Because of their complicated anatomy, it is medically impossible to separate them. They likely wouldn't want that anyway. But they are two very unique and independent young women. Abby is described as the more outgoing of the two, while Brittany is a little on the shy side. They both like different foods, different colors, different television shows. And if there wasn't a lot of compromise thrown into the mix, there'd be sibling rivalry like never before.

The girls live on the family farm in Minnesota and attend a small Christian school. But even though they share a lot of their anatomy, they still have to study, write assignments and take tests independently. The TLC documentary entitled *Joined for Life: Abby & Brittany Turn 16* celebrated their milestone birthday, following up on an earlier documentary entitled *Abby & Brittany: Joined for Life*. Both documentaries demonstrated how the girls work independently of one another in some situations and together, almost as a single unit, in others—such as when they were learning to drive and had to decide who was responsible for what. Incidentally, they each had to take and pass their own individual driver's tests before getting their licenses.

Whether walking, running, riding a bicycle or playing sports, these young women take part in it all. And even though each twin can't feel sensation on the other side of her body, they instinctively act as one. If you ask them how they do it, they wouldn't have a complete explanation for you. It's just how they live.

There are only four known cases of dicephalus twins surviving infancy. So far, Abby and Brittany have lived a healthy life. With all the love and support of their family and surrounding community, there's little doubt that will continue to be the case.

Inspiration to a Nation

On February 26, 2002, the University of Utah Medical Center in Salt Lake City, Utah, witnessed the miracle of birth. You might say that's quite a common miracle, but baby girls Kendra Deene and Maliyah Mae Herrin are one in many million. The identical twins were born as ischiopagus-omphalopagus conjoined twins, joined at the abdomen and pelvis. They also shared a liver, a kidney and a large intestine.

The girls went through separation surgery when they were four and a half. The single kidney they shared remained with Kendra, and Maliyah survived on hemodialysis treatments until she was well enough to undergo a transplant operation. The twins' mother, Erin, donated one of her kidneys for the procedure.

Life hasn't been uneventful since the twins' separation. Both girls have experienced health issues, and their parents Erin and Jake continue to work hard and pray hard for their daughters' ongoing recovery.

Triple Threat

There is some evidence that the occurrence of conjoined triplets is possible, but it appears the cases on record refer to a child born with parasitic siblings. The most cited reference is that of a boy in Italy who, in 1831, was born with three heads. There have also been reports of triplet births in which two of the triplets are conjoined.

- On September 24, 1981, Jeanette, Jillian and Jacklyn Barcena were born to Bertha and Armondo in El Paso, Texas. Jeanette and Jillian were born conjoined and only lived for a month, but the last news report on this family stated baby Jacklyn went home and was, at that time, doing well.

- In November 2007, Reuters reported the birth of triplets in north China's Tianjin municipality. The siblings included conjoined twin boys, Liu Tianyu and Liu Yuxuan, and a little girl. The Beijing News reported that after a four-hour surgery to separate them on February 16, 2008, the boys were doing fine and their prognosis as promising as any other babies their age. Thankfully, the boys were joined only at the waist, and their spines and organs were separate.

DID YOU KNOW?

Although the instance of conjoined twins is the direct result of the incomplete division of an egg, which typically occurs early on in a pregnancy, accurate diagnosis isn't usually reliable until the last trimester of pregnancy.

TRADITIONAL BIRTHING METHODS

Giving birth is the most uniquely feminine thing a woman can do. Throughout the ages, the act of childbearing automatically propelled a female into an entirely different status in her community. Women unable to conceive and bear children were often, sadly, scorned by the other women in their company—and likely by their mates. Prior to the

*development of modern medicine, it never occurred to folks
that a woman's inability to conceive might be related to a
medical problem with her mate and not her own anatomy.
Regardless, that's how societies once viewed this part of
life—and it was fairly similar across cultural lines. Of
course, today it's not at all uncommon for women to choose
not to have children. But for those of us for whom having a
baby is still something we want to experience, here's a look
at how our ancestors did it.*

Russian Birthing Bania

A special bathhouse used for saunas or steam baths during
important periods in a person's life was called the *bania* in the
Russian tradition. Birth was one of those occasions when the
bania was used. It was a place of healing, but all was not smooth
sailing here. The *bania* was the domain of the Bannik, and
though he was usually a temperate spirit, if he was angered, he'd
lash out for inappropriate behavior. To keep the Bannik happy, a
regular firing of the bathhouse was offered to him.

The *bania* was a perfect healing place for a woman to give birth,
as long as the midwife was there to keep things in order.
Charms or magical spells were chanted to protect the mother
during her labor, and the mother herself often repeated the
charms after the birth.

Sauna Comfort

Finnish women also traditionally took advantage of the sauna
during childbirth. Until well into the 1900s, and the advance of
modern medical techniques, Finnish women who were able
almost uniformly took to the sauna when their time to deliver
came. It was believed the warmth of the sauna was purifying
and helped defend against bacteria, protecting both mother and
child from infection.

Cradleboards

Caring for a baby is pretty much a full-time endeavor, but let's face it—there are other chores that need doing on any given day. In order to tend to those jobs but at the same time ensure baby was safe, North American Native mothers created the cradleboard. Cradleboards were flat pieces of wood, often with a slightly hollowed center for a more comfortable fit. Cloth or some type of animal skin was attached to the board and laced up the center to secure baby inside. Different tribes had different rituals associated with the making of cradleboards. In one tradition, the board had to be started at dawn and completed before dusk—that included any ornamental embellishments. If the job was successfully completed in one day, it meant the child would grow up to be a good person. Just as with strollers and baby seats today, cradleboards often included a halo-shaped hoop suspended in front of baby with little trinkets attached to amuse the youngster when mama had to lay her baby down for a while.

Newborns were kept bundled in the baby board until they were weaned and able to walk on their own. However, another tradition firmly believed that the baby, and not the mother, decided when it was time to leave the baby board.

DID YOU KNOW?

To increase the odds of having an attractive baby, some Japanese take to cleaning toilets. That's because they believe humbling themselves in this way will increase the chances of having a pretty baby. And if you don't want a spoiled baby, don't let friends and family members rub your pregnant belly.

Welcome to the Family, Mama
In the Kenyan tradition, a newly married woman isn't fully integrated into her husband's family unit until she is pregnant. And while she's pregnant, she's considered "ritually unclean" and

doesn't have any contact with her husband—not even to cook and clean for him—until the baby is born. Once the big day finally arrives, and baby is born, the mother is instructed to scream five times if the child is a boy and four if it is a girl. The umbilical cord and placenta, the sacred bond between the mother and child, is taken away and buried in an uncultivated field in order to break that sacred connection. That way, the child can enter into a world in which mother and father hold equal significance.

DID YOU KNOW?

The meaning behind a name is the most important thing about naming a child in many traditional African countries. In fact, the circumstances on the day of the baby's birth should have some bearing on choosing the name. For example, if the child has his or her grandfather's eyes, and the grandfather is recently deceased, the child may take that name. And if it was sunny or raining on the day of the birth, the name should somehow reflect that.

A List of Names

In Somalian families, children are given three names. The first name is often specially picked for the child, but is sometimes the name of a grandparent; the child's second name is usually the father's name; and the paternal grandfather's name is the third name.

Polish Names

A lot of Polish names are very nearly unisex—with one exception. All female names end with an *a*. For example, a male child would be named "Stanislaw," and a female child would be named "Stanislawa."

Making the Right Choice
Islamic children who show a preference for left-handedness are encouraged to use their right hand—it's considered the polite choice.

DID YOU KNOW?

A Danish birthday cake is called a *lagkage*.

Long, Lovely Locks
Filipinos believe that if you want a child with a lot of hair right from birth, try keeping a healthy dose of eggplant in your diet.

Silver and Gold

It's a common and long-standing practice among many European cultures—such as the Greeks and Ukrainians—to give silver coins (or gold, if you have them) to newborns. It's believed this will bring luck and prosperity to their future.

Evil Eye
A *mati*—a small blue stone with a black center—is often given to Greek newborns to ward off the "evil eye." Another charm is a pouch containing crushed, dried Easter flowers.

DID YOU KNOW?

In some ancient societies, the birth of twins and triplets was a feared event. These children were usually treated very differently from other youngsters, and in some cases they were even put to death.

Dodging the Devil

Talking about scaring the life out of your newborn! The folks down in Spain have a rather hands-on, albeit frightening, way of keeping the devil at bay when it comes to harming their babies. Since 1620, folks in that part of the world have dressed someone up as a devil, placed their babies on the ground and encouraged the makeshift devil to leap over their youngsters.

The practice, known as *El Colacho*, takes place during the annual Corpus Christi celebration in the village of Castrillo de Murcia, and these strangely attired men are called "Jumping Devils." Now if that doesn't produce a little separation anxiety in these youngsters, I'm not sure what will.

TURKISH DELIGHT

There's an old Turkish superstition that says if a woman eats bitter food during her pregnancy, she's "doomed" to have a girl, but if she has a sweet tooth her baby is sure to be a boy—or, as the saying goes, "Eat sweet things and give birth to a cavalryman."

If you're a traditionalist of this ethnic background, here is a list of explicit dos and don'ts for expectant mothers. It is believed that following these practices will ensure you'll have a (relatively) easy birth and a happy baby.

Watch What You Look At!

If you live in an area where there's a prevalence of bears, monkeys or camels, you shouldn't look at them. Don't look at any dead people either, and don't even think of attending a funeral!

Culinary Etiquette

Don't talk or eat in secret, and don't chew gum, or eat fish, rabbit, trotters or sheep's heads. You should, however, eat quinces, apples, green plums and grapes.

Take in Life's Beauty

Stop to smell the roses, look at the moon or just watch the beautiful people pass by. Infusing your mind with good, positive images will send good feelings to the growing baby inside you.

Once Labor Starts

A midwife or other women attending a traditional Turkish childbirth might employ one or more of the following procedures, each of which have been credited with helping ease labor:

☞ Someone is sent out to feed the birds.

☞ All hairclips or ties are removed from the laboring mother's hair. As well, any locked doors, closets, windows or other items are opened. Perhaps the symbolism here is to eliminate any constrictions and allow for a better flow throughout the room, thereby getting rid of any obstacles to the impending birth.

☞ A swatch of cloth is laid on the ground and the laboring mother is invited to sit there while the midwife gently rocks her.

☞ If the woman is having a particularly difficult time, a friend or relative who has had an easy birth is sent for. This person then rubs the laboring mother's back.

Once Baby Arrives

The Turkish tradition has several intricate procedures following a birth. Many of these customs deal with disposing of the umbilical cord and placenta, while others largely focus on the mother and baby during "accouchement." This 40-day period following the birth is when the mother is believed to be in danger from various supernatural forces, and protecting the mother and baby from a "mother-snatcher" or "baby-snatcher" is crucial.

Planning for the Future

There's a lot of ceremony around the disposal of the umbilical cord and placenta. In the Turkish tradition, it is believed that caring for what was once baby's lifeline will secure it a happy, healthy, successful and prosperous future. In order to achieve a specifically desired result, prescribed procedures are outlined. For example, if the baby was born to a family of farmers or veterinarians, the child's love for animals would be a good thing. To ensure this happens, that baby's umbilical cord would be buried in a stable. If you're hoping for junior to be a scholar, bury the cord in a school garden. If you want a devout child, the cord should be buried near a mosque, and if you hope for adventure and travel in your child's future, throw the cord into the water.

Extra Care Needed
The placenta, on the other hand, is considered an extension of the living baby and is swaddled in a clean cloth and buried with great care and ceremony.

Dangerous Proposition

Because childbearing is probably one of the most potentially dangerous experiences a woman can go through, before the advent of modern medicine, it wasn't uncommon for women to die during or shortly after having a baby. Likewise, the first few days of a newborn's life were also incredibly worrisome. Perhaps this is where the mother- and/or baby-snatcher concerns stemmed from. To protect newly lactating moms and their babes, women in accouchement were closely monitored for 40 days, were not allowed out and especially were not allowed to mingle with other mothers and babies in accouchement.

Falling Forties
If mother and babe struggle to regain their strength in the critical 40-day period after the birth, it is called the "falling forties."

DID YOU KNOW?

A Turkish woman who's just given birth can be given any one of six traditional names: *logusa, lohsa, emzikli, logsa, nevse* or *kirkli*.

CHINESE TRADITIONS

In a land full of custom and tradition, it's no surprise that the most important thing a woman will ever do in her life is influenced by many traditions for the Chinese.

The Importance of Custom

Following the traditional wedding celebrations of a new couple, and before they've even had time to consummate their marriage, the new groom must carry his bride over a pan of burning coals before entering their new home. This is meant to ensure the new bride will pass through labor successfully.

Once the new bride becomes pregnant, no more sexual intimacy occurs between her and her beloved until the baby is born. The Chinese believe everything influences the growing fetus—all thoughts and emotions will pass down to the child's heart and mind. Therefore, the expectant mother must be cautious in every aspect of her life.

Recipe for a Happy Baby

In the Chinese tradition, a pregnant woman must read good poetry and thoughtful books, activities that will help her child develop a thoughtful and intelligent disposition. She must maintain proper decorum at all times, never laughing out loud, gossiping or losing her temper—behaviors that only provide the growing infant with negative feelings. She also shouldn't look at anything that's displeasing—such as a "crooked mat."

You Are What You Eat
For the Chinese, a pregnant woman's diet must be impeccably maintained. Food should be visually appealing and properly cut. Consuming a hastily prepared meal could instill a "careless disposition" in the unborn child. If a lot of light-colored foods

are consumed during pregnancy, it's believed the baby will be fair-skinned. Eat too many spicy foods, and your baby is sure to have a temper or develop colic—one of the two.

Too Much of a Good Thing?

Although it's not uncommon to see pregnant women everywhere lovingly rubbing their bellies, the Chinese warn against doing it too much. That action does pass the good feelings of love and affection felt by the mother onto the baby, but too much rubbing could result in a very demanding child, or so the traditional way of thinking goes.

What's Under Your Bed?

You might get a fright looking under the bed of a traditional Chinese mother-to-be. That's because knives are often placed under the bed of a pregnant woman in an effort to protect her from any evil spirits that might attack her.

A Unique Mobile?

If you have a bunch of toddlers about and fear that leaving sharp objects under your bed could result in a nasty situation, try hanging paper cutouts in the shape of scissors from the curtain rod or hanging tiger pelts over the bed. It's believed the cutouts are just as threatening to the evil spirits and will protect you from any potential attack.

Easing the Pain

Traditionally, the Chinese believe a woman's career is childbearing, and she must never fear the experience. Instead, she can do specific things to help minimize her pain, such as drinking strong, herbal tea during labor. A comfortable armchair, where she will sit during the majority of her labor, is also prepared for her comfort. And once the baby is born, prayers are said.

Don't Get Carried Away

Having a baby shower before baby is born is warned against—it could bring bad luck for the baby. However, about a month before the baby's due date, the maternal grandmother will prepare a *tsue shen*—a package of clothing and other goodies for both mother and child. Included in the *tsue shen* is a new white cloth that the newborn will be wrapped in.

Taking Precautions

Once the big day finally arrives, a fortune-teller is often sought for advice on the child's future. Because the Chinese believe each of us is made up of some amount of earth, wind, fire, water and metal, the fortune-teller will determine if the new baby is missing any of these elements. If so, the child's middle name will reflect the missing element in some way.

Which Name?

In the Chinese tradition, a baby is never named before birth. To do so is nothing short of tempting fate and inviting bad luck. A fake name is sometimes used, however. This confuses any evil spirits that may be lurking about, looking to kidnap the newborn. Another effort at discouraging these spirits often used by Chinese parents is to call their unborn baby ugly or worthless—even an evil spirit isn't interested in a "worthless" baby.

The name game doesn't end there. A Chinese child could conceivably have several names during his or her lifetime—a birth name, a new name upon entering school, another name after graduation, and perhaps even a final name will be given after death.

Bells and Whistles

If all this wasn't discouraging enough for any lurking demons, once a baby is born, a ribbon adorned with golden bells is gently tied to each ankle and wrist to keep away any persistent bad spirits. Apparently, the bells either alert baby's parents that something is going on, or else evil spirits don't like the sound of bells.

I Can See Them

Chinese parents with children who demonstrate a slightly anxious disposition must be biting their nails to the quick. Chinese superstition states that nervous children are often that way because they are able to see the evil spirits. Bet that would scare you, too!

Color Is the Key

Red is an important color when it comes to dealing with these devilish kidnappers. Red pouches stuffed with a red powdery substance called vermilion are often pinned to the child's clothes.

Eye of the Tiger

Little boys, so desperately coveted in the Chinese culture, need extra protection and often have tigers sewn or embroidered onto their shoes.

Sit Back and Take It Easy

After baby is born, the mother spends the first month in bed and caters to her newborn. This is called "sit the month." In extremely traditional households, even her husband is discouraged from seeing her. She often doesn't shower for a full week, and when she does, she rinses her hair in ginger water.

First Bath

The new baby is bathed for the first time on day three. Hot water is prepared with locust branches and artemisia plants and placed into a special tub. The bed is rapped in a red bow, and "a straw sieve, a padlock, an onion, a comb and a weight" are placed strategically around the mother, midwife, baby and tub. Guests arrive with special gifts, red envelops with money and coins, as well as bits of fruit that are placed in the bath water. It's one of the most elaborate "first baths."

Special Celebration

Once baby is one month old, it is a long-standing Chinese tradition—one that's still practiced today, even among modern families—to hold a party for the baby. In a way, it's almost a coming-out party for mom, too, since a month of confinement and diligent personal care is also something many modern Chinese mothers still do. Friends and family gather together for the rather formal festivities. This celebration is one of the largest held for the newborn. Among the more unusual ceremonial components of the event is that the tongue of a cooked chicken is rubbed along the baby's lips. Tradition dictates this will make the child a good talker.

Happy 100 Days!

Every new baby has countless developmental milestones during its first 100 days outside the womb, and the Chinese have a special way of celebrating these firsts. On baby's 100th day, family and friends gather together, once again, to celebrate. This 100th-day celebration includes a feast of fish and chicken, and the child's paternal grandfather will sometimes present a rocking chair to the mother.

Happy Birthday, Chinese Style

A birthday bash bar none is celebrated when a Chinese infant turns one year old. Among the many symbolic tokens gifted to the birthday child is a gold ring. This ring is supposed to "protect the baby during harsh times." A feast is prepared and offered up to the gods, and the child is presented with a *yu char kuei* or "long bread." It's believed this will help baby learn to walk.

Breaking the Ties

Around the time baby begins to walk, the Chinese have a very interesting tradition that follows immediately after a child's first independent steps. Whichever relative happens to be around during the big event will take a knife and make three lines on the ground. This action is meant to sever the child's present life from any attachment to previous lives, and the child is left to walk the rest of his or her days freely.

HEBREW CUSTOMS

All life is precious, but in many cultures, newborn sons get special treatment. Aside from the social excitement that surrounds such an event, the Jewish tradition celebrates several milestones in a young boy's life in very significant ways. The Jewish tradition is also unique in that over its recent history, new celebrations of equal importance have been incorporated for families of newborn girls.

Welcoming a Son

The first right of passage a baby boy of the Jewish faith goes through is circumcision, called the bris. A mohel, a person specially trained to perform ritual Jewish circumcisions, must perform this ceremony on the baby's eighth day of life. The only reason for a delay would be if the child was suffering some health issues.

Receiving Redemption

Another rather crucial ceremony, although not applicable to all baby boys of the Jewish faith, is the Pidyon Haben. While only performed in select instances, it is actually one of the largest ceremonies of its kind.

The Pidyon Haben, also known as the Redemption of the Firstborn Son, is held after a married couple of the Jewish faith (neither of whom can be a descendant of Levi or Aaron) welcomes their firstborn son into the world through a vaginal birth. The couple must not have had a previous son by cesarean, nor could they have experienced any miscarriages. The ceremony, which involves five silver coins and a series of prayers in the presence of 10 men, takes place when baby is 29 and a half days old. (Some sources state the ceremony is to be held on the child's 31st day.)

This redemption hails back to the time when the firstborn sons liberated from Egypt were deemed holy and expected to become priests of the holy temple. But during their sojourn in the desert, when Moses was on the mountain, the people became restless and turned to worshipping the Golden Calf. Their "holy" status therefore was tarnished for all time, hence the need for redemption.

Only one in 10 firstborn sons is believed to meet all the criteria for a Pidyon Haben. In some cases, a boy who meets the requirements of the ceremony is overlooked. Should that occur, there is no need to panic. An adult firstborn male can take the responsibility of organizing his own Pidyon Haben.

Two Names

Jewish parents have a lot to consider when naming their baby. They need to find an everyday name that suits their tastes. But they also have to choose a Hebrew name for their youngster— and there are a few dos and don'ts when it comes to that process. Most Jewish families will choose to honor a deceased relative in the naming of their child. That doesn't necessarily mean using the same name over again. Instead, they might choose the first letter of that relative's name and pick another name that starts with that letter. Children are never named after a father or grandfather if that person is still alive. The Jewish tradition believes doing this will rob the living family member of a full life—the little one will take it over.

Once names are chosen, prayers and a reading of the Torah are held at the family's home on the first Friday night following the baby's birth.

Brit Bat

With so many important rituals revolving around the birth of a boy, ceremonies to celebrate the birth of a daughter were sadly lacking in several traditions, and the ones that were in place weren't routinely practiced. More recently, Jewish families have started celebrating the Simchat Bat ("Joy of a Daughter") or Brit Habat ("Covenant of the Daughter"). Some of the ceremonial rituals of the big day were the same as those conducted during a boy's bris, minus the circumcision, of course. Along with a family feast, the baby is officially named, prayers of thanksgiving are offered, and the baby girl's feet are ceremonially washed.

KOREAN PREFERENCES

Boy, Oh Boy!

Having a boy child is important in many cultures, but a traditional Korean family might take the process a step further. If a woman wasn't able to conceive a son, her mother-in-law often chose a surrogate mother. That woman's sole job was to try to produce a son.

Praying for Protection

In the Korean tradition, a prayer for the child's protection, called the Avalokiteshvara, is recited while the baby makes its way through the birth canal. The prayer is recited again after the birth to protect the child throughout life.

Focused Prayer

Korean mothers also pray to the San-shin goddess (or grandmother spirit) during their pregnancy. These prayers are specifically tailored to a request for a boy baby, as well as ongoing protection.

Checking Out the Situation

The responsibility for overseeing the birthing process in the Korean tradition goes to the mother-in-law. One of her main responsibilities is to ensure that tradition is followed to the letter.

Strong and Stoic

Women are forbidden to scream or show pain during childbirth. In the Korean tradition, and indeed many modern religions such as Scientology, this is seen as a sign of weakness that will be passed on to the infant.

Post-Labor Cuisine
During the traditional 21-day confinement, the new mother is only fed warm foods and drinks. In particular, a seaweed soup called *miyuk guk* is prepared for her. It's a natural detox believed to cleanse any toxins accumulated during childbirth from the woman's body.

No Visitors Allowed
Only the family visits a newborn for its first 100 days of life. Then, similar to the Chinese tradition of the one-month-old and the 100th-day parties for babies, Korean parents host a *baek-il* celebration. Prayers are said to the three-spirit San-shin god in the hope of bringing the child wealth, health, luck and longevity.

The Power of Touch

Korean parents believe that massaging their baby's legs will help the child grow strong and tall. Massaging the eyelids to help baby develop eye folds is a newer tradition.

Planning for the Future

Because the mortality rate of newborns was so high in ancient times, if babies saw their first birthday, a huge celebration, called a *toi*, was held. Prayers, gifts and a feast, as always, were part of the festivities, but modern Koreans have added a unique twist to the first-birthday tradition. Parents surround the youngster with items, such as a cooking utensil, a pencil or a hammer, and whichever item the baby grabs for is believed to be the child's chosen career.

PAGAN BIRTHING TRADITIONS

Throughout the ages, a general respect and value was typically given to the cultural, religious and ethnic practices surrounding important milestones in a person's life, such as having a baby. But pre-Christian era, polytheistic pagan traditions were often historically viewed as circumspect. Misconceptions surrounding pagan beliefs and practices continue on some level; however, today's society is far more accepting than it once was. For the practicing pagan, birth is a monumental event. Here are just some of that religion's birthing rituals.

In the Beginning

Once a practicing pagan woman decides she wants to get pregnant, a birth altar is often the first order of business. Along with a Mother-Goddess statue, family pictures, valued heirlooms and herbs believed to aid the mother through pregnancy and childbirth are placed on the altar. Other articles are added throughout the pregnancy, such as a special item purchased for the child or items from the mother's or father's infancy. As well, if your growing belly wasn't advertisement enough, adding a plant or scattering seeds over the alter some time in the second trimester of the pregnancy provides a visible sign of the new life growing inside the woman.

Going Natural

Herbs such as primrose, red clover and nettle leaves can also be hung over the pregnant woman's bed, or the herbs are placed inside the pillowcase or under the bed.

DID YOU KNOW?

Pregnant women sometimes wear knotted cords around their wrist, ankle or neck, or place the cord under the bed to aid in fertility.

A Clean Sweep

A broom, also used at pagan wedding ceremonies, is believed to be a symbol of fertility as well and is placed somewhere in the house or, again, under the bed. If a broom wasn't used at the wedding ceremony, a new one is purchased, or a silver charm in the shape of a broom can also be worn.

Shine a Little Light

A lit candle should be nearby during labor to help "light the way" to delivery. Friends and family members of the woman's spiritual group are also encouraged to light candles.

He Shall Be Called

Once baby is about a month or so old, many pagans hold a naming ceremony. This allows the parents to share their birthing story and gives friends and family a chance to welcome the little one.

A Spiritual Name

Children in the pagan tradition are usually given two names—one for everyday use, and one that's only used in the family circle or spiritual group.

Looking to the Stars

It's also common for parents in the pagan tradition to have their baby's astrological chart done up. This is then used as a tool in deciding on the best parenting methods for the child.

HAPPY BIRTHDAY BABY

*If you're an expectant mother who has tried for a long time
to have a baby, chances are you've been celebrating
the birth since you found out you were pregnant. So when it
comes time to actually throw junior's first birthday bash,
it's likely a no-holds-barred occasion. In that first year,
you've traveled through more stages, witnessed more changes
and marveled at more of your little one's developments than
you will during any other year in his or her life. It's only*

*right you should celebrate! But who was it that originally
baked the first birthday cake, lit the first birthday candle or
started the tradition of making a wish as you blew the
candle out? Historians don't necessarily agree, but here
are a few of the theories.*

Gastronomical Greeks
Blame it on the Greeks. That's one theory, anyhow. Some historians suggest the round honey cakes of Greek tradition, baked specially for the moon goddess, Artemis, were used as the first birthday cakes.

Not Just for Baby

Personal birthdays weren't the only birthdays recognized in ancient Rome. Communities held annual galas for their cities and temples. And they religiously celebrated the birthdays of members of an imperial family.

A Simple Bread
Sweetened bread dough shaped into the form of baby Jesus is a German convention that some historians suggest may have also started the tradition of birthday cakes.

Hidden Treasures

Inserting trinkets into birthday cakes was an old German tradition that began centuries ago. The trinkets were symbolic and were used to tell the birthday guests' futures.

In Search of the Future

During medieval times in England, coins and thimbles were actually baked into a cake, but the reason behind this custom was the same—to tell someone's future. If you discovered a coin in your piece of cake, you could look forward to prosperity, but if you found a thimble, your future was a little less bright—you would have a lonely life without the joys of marriage to look forward to.

Lighting the Flame

It's unclear where the tradition of lighting candles on the birthday cake came from. Some historians point to the Germans, who sometime during the Age of Enlightenment added a central "light of life" candle to the top of their child's birthday cake. But if you dig further back in history, the ancient Greeks and Romans prayed to their gods over flames and the rising smoke.

Perhaps this earlier religious tradition, combined with the newer practice of lighting a birthday candle, is what started the "make a wish" tradition while the candles burn on the cake. Regardless, it's a tradition we all love!

Take a Deep Breath
It's a North American tradition that if all the candles on the cake are blown out with one breath, your wish will come true.

DID YOU KNOW?

Sears Roebuck first offered birthday candles for sale in their catalog in 1927.

The First Cut
In many families, the birthday girl or guy gets to slice into the birthday cake first. It's commonly believed this tradition began in North America.

Musical Credits

The first documented record of the song and tune to "Happy Birthday to You" dates back to 1912 America. Back in the 1890s, two kindergarten teachers, Mildred and Patti Hill, from Louisville, Kentucky, were credited with creating the "Happy Birthday" tune—the melody was originally paired with a song the sisters wrote titled "Good Morning to All." One source suggests that 40 years later, Patti wrote the lyrics to the "Happy Birthday" song, while another version of the story tells of how the students so enjoyed the original tune that the sisters started using it to sing a birthday greeting to them. When the song began receiving such widespread attention that it even made it into movies, another sister, Jessica Hill, had it copyrighted. That copyright doesn't expire until 2030, which technically speaking, means that unless you're paying royalties, you shouldn't be singing "Happy Birthday" in a public place.

Special Birthdays

Many cultures around the world bestow different significance on different milestone birthdays. For example, in the Filipino culture, 18 and 65 are especially important birthdays, but they pale in comparison to a child's first birthday. Unless finances place restrictions on the event, there's almost no limit to the elaborate party held. A hall is often rented, hundreds of guests are invited and regal clothes are purchased for the one-year-old. I've even heard recent stories of the little prince or princess being brought to their special celebration in a horse-drawn carriage or a limousine. The party usually goes well into the night, far past the time the little one has finally fallen asleep.

Symbolic Food

Noodles are usually served at a child's birthday party in the Chinese tradition. The noodles symbolize long life.

Thankful Reverence

Birthdays are religious celebrations in the Hindu tradition. The child visits the temple, presenting the priest with a gift of flowers and asking for a blessing. Birthdays in this culture are only celebrated for the first 16 years.

One for Good Luck

The Irish are credited with starting the birthday "bumps" ritual, while families in Israel place a child on a chair and raise the chair into the air the same number of times as the child's birthday year. In each tradition, one extra bump or chair-raising is done for good luck.

DID YOU  KNOW?

Smashing piñatas to get to the candy is a Mexican custom that dates back at least 300 years. It rains candy for youngsters from that tradition.

THOUGHTFUL QUOTES

Everyone loves a baby. It's a deep thought, and—wait a minute—it's also a famous quote. Although my research doesn't provide a single source for this particular quote, I believe it is one of those long-standing sayings that are passed on through the ages.

Variations on "everyone loves a baby" can be found in everything from the title of an episode of the 1971 television series Budgie *("Everybody Loves a Baby") starring Adam Faith and Iain Cuthbertson, to songs such as "Everybody Loves Me Baby" by Don McLean and "Everybody Loves My Baby" by Jack Palmer and Spencer Williams. You get the idea. Everyone loves a baby, and if there was ever any doubt, just read through the selection of quotes listed here. They'll leave you with a lot to think about.*

"A baby will make love stronger, days shorter, nights longer, bankroll smaller, home happier, clothes shabbier, the past forgotten, and the future worth living for."

–Anonymous

"It is a pleasant thing to reflect upon, and furnishes a complete answer to those who contend for the gradual degeneration of the human species, that every baby born into the world is a finer one than the last."

–Charles Dickens, writer

"A baby is an inestimable blessing and bother."

–Mark Twain, writer

"A baby is an angel whose wings decrease as his legs increase."

–Anonymous

"A baby is God's opinion that life should go on."

–Carl Sandburg, writer, historian and critic

"If one feels the need of something grand, something infinite, something that makes one feel aware of God, one need not go far to find it. I think that I see something deeper, more infinite, more eternal than the ocean in the expression of the eyes of a little baby when it wakes in the morning and coos or laughs because it sees the sun shining on its cradle."

–Vincent Van Gogh, artist

"When the first baby laughed for the first time, the laugh broke into a thousand pieces and they all went skipping about, and that was the beginning of fairies. And now when every new baby is born, its first laugh becomes a fairy."

–James Matthew Barrie, dramatist and author of *Peter Pan*

"Babies are such a nice way to start people."

–Don Herold, cartoonist

"Ten fingers, ten toes.
She's laughter and teardrops.
So small and brand new,
And amazingly angelic.
She's sent to bless you.
She's one special baby.
The best of life's treasure,
And will grant and bless you
Many hours of great pleasure."

–Anonymous

"Making the decision to have a child is momentous. It is to decide forever to have your heart go walking around outside your body."

–Elizabeth Stone, writer and photographer

"A new baby is like the beginning of all things—wonder, hope, a dream of possibilities."

–Eda J. Le Shan, psychologist and family counselor

FUNNY QUOTES

If you've ever had a baby—or if you ever hope to have one—here's a piece of advice for you to chew on: you've got to have a sense of humor. For those days when baby is crying incessantly and you haven't even had a chance to pee in the last 12 hours, here are a few quirky quotes to tuck away in your memory bank. They'll get you laughing...of course, then you'll really need the bathroom.

"Diaper backwards spells repaid. Think about it."

–Marshall McLuhan, writer, philosopher and scholar

"Think of stretch marks as pregnancy service stripes."

–Joyce Armor, writer

"Parents are the bones on which children cut their teeth."

–Peter Ustinov, actor

"People who say they sleep like a baby usually don't have one."

–Leo J. Burke, writer

"Before I got married I had six theories about bring up children; now I have six children and no theories."

–John Wilmot, politician

"Babies haven't any hair; ole men's heads are just as bare; between the cradle and the grave lie a haircut and a shave."

–Samuel Hoffenstein, screenwriter and composer

"My mother says I didn't open my eyes for eight days after I was born, but when I did, the first thing I saw was an engagement ring. I was hooked."

—Elizabeth Taylor, actress

"If your baby is beautiful and perfect, never cries or fusses, sleeps on schedule and burps on demand, an angel all the time, you're the grandma."

—Theresa Bloomingdale, writer

"Giving birth is like taking your lower lip and forcing it over your head."

—Carol Burnett, actress and comedian

"Women say…that if men had to have babies there would soon be no babies in the world…I have sometimes wished that some clever man would actually have a baby in some new labour-saving way; then all men could take it up, and one of the oldest taunts in the world would be stilled forever."

–Robertson Davies, writer

"A child is a curly haired, dimpled lunatic."

–Ralph Waldo Emerson, writer

"Having a baby changes the way you view your in-laws. I love it when they come to visit now. They can hold the baby and I can go out."

–Matthew Broderick, actor

"A baby changes your dinner party conversation from politics to poops."

–Maurice Johnstone, composer

CELEBRITY QUOTES

You might have said it. I may have said it. But when someone from Hollywood says it, IT makes the news!

"I don't know yet if we are having a boy or a girl, but I'm excited that I have a life inside me that my husband and I created."

> –Laila Ali, professional boxer, in the March 26, 2008, edition of *Essence* magazine, commenting on expecting her first child with hubby Curtis Conway. The couple later had a baby boy on August 26, 2008.

"My butt getting bigger is so not important when there's a human being rolling around in my tummy that's half of me and half of Cash. Weight is not the most important thing in the world."

> –Jessica Alba, actress, in the May 12, 2008, issue of *People*

"I didn't know how babies were made until I was pregnant with my fourth child."

> –Loretta Lynn, singer

"I have no problem with people putting their hands on my tummy without asking. I like the contact and connection."

> –Nicole Kidman, actress, in the May 12, 2008, issue of *People*

"[Breastfeeding] is very time consuming, it really is a labor of love. It depends on the child, too. Because Lola and Michael were great eaters. But Joaquin really took his time and was like 'Mom, I think we should see other people.' And he still, like to this day, is a fussy eater."

> –Kelly Ripa, actress and talk-show host, during a conversation with Regis Philbin on *Live with Regis and Kelly*

"Is there ever a perfect time? A baby's always going to interrupt something, isn't it?"

–Madonna, singer

"I just looked at her and said, 'Chelsea, you've never been a baby before, and I've never been a mother before, and we're just going to have to help each other get through this.'"

–Hillary Rodham Clinton, 2008
presidential candidate

"There are no strictly Dad duties or Mom duties except giving birth and breastfeeding."

–Jada Pinkett Smith, actress and singer

"We're being surprised [at the delivery]. I would be pleased with either [sex].

–Keri Russell, actress, in the May 14, 2007, issue of *People*

"All the secrets from your family come out of the closet for some reason [when you're pregnant]. But it's good. They have to come out sometime. You know what I mean?"

–Britney Spears, singer, in the September 9, 2005,
issue of *People Magazine Online*

SING IT TO ME, BABY

Over the years, the word "baby" has come to mean more than just the infant of our species—it's taken its place alongside other popular terms of endearment such as "sweetheart," "honey," "kitten," "sugarcakes" and…well, you get the idea. Incidentally, if you're planning a baby shower and looking for a fun game, why not ask your guests to write down the titles of as many popular songs as they can think of with the word "baby" in them. Set a timer and see what everyone comes up with.

Can't Get Enough

Gus Kahn, inspired by a young girl's toy, wrote the lyrics to the adult song "Yes Sir, That's My Baby" in the 1920s. Ace Brigode first recorded it in 1925, and since then more than 50 additional recordings have been released.

Private Practice

Composer and lyricist Frank Loesser wrote the song "Baby, It's Cold Outside" in 1944, and the first time it was ever heard was when he performed it with his wife at a housewarming party. He sold the rights to the song to MGM in 1948, and it was used in the movie *Neptune's Daughter* the following year. The song was performed twice in the movie and earned Loesser an Academy Award for Best Original Song. More than three dozen different artists have since recorded it over the years.

Believe in Yourself

In 1960, Rosie & the Originals recorded "Angel Baby." Rosie was only 15 at the time the single was recorded, and the group had a hard time finding a label willing to back them. But when the song was finally released, it peaked at number five on the Billboard Hot 100 chart and stayed there for 12 weeks.

More Than Just a Song

"Baby, Let Me Hold Your Hand," released in 1951, was Ray Charles' second hit with Swingtime Records. Charles is also credited with popularizing the Pepsi slogan "You Got the Right One, Baby."

DID YOU KNOW?

Carole King and Gerry Goffin wrote the song "Take Good Care of My Baby." It hit number one on the Billboard Hot 100 in 1961, thanks in part to the vocal strength of Bobby Vee. A few years later, in 1968, after being re-recorded by another Bobby—Bobby Vinton—it again registered on the charts, this time topping out at number 33.

Big One, Baby

Henry Mancini wrote "Baby Elephant Walk" in 1961 for the movie *Hatari!* The song become one of Mancini's most recognizable tunes and has been used in countless commercials, game shows and skits since then. According to one source, Lawrence Welk helped propel this little ditty into the public spotlight. Meanwhile, critics of *Hatari!* consider "Baby Elephant Walk" the only "memorable" part of the movie.

Like Fine Wine

In 1963, The Drifters recorded "Ruby Baby." The song, written by Jerry Leiber and Mike Stoller, was a hit when it was originally released, and it continued to produce good results for other artists, including Dion (1963), Billy "Crash" Craddock (1974) and The Beach Boys (1993), among others.

Winning Combination

The trio of Phil Spector, Jeff Barry and Ellie Greenwich wrote "Be My Baby" in 1963. Performed by the Ronettes, the song quickly became a number one hit. It was listed 22nd on the Rolling Stone's 500 Greatest Songs of All Time list, made it into the Grammy Hall of Fame in 1999 and was even recognized by the Library of Congress in 2006.

Good Around the Globe

Another Ronettes single, "Baby I Love You," made it to number 24 on the American Billboard chart in 1964. According to the UK charts, where it hit number 11, the Brits were also fond of the song. The team of Spector, Barry and Greenwich were again the masterminds behind this hit single.

Yearning for Love

"Baby I Need Your Loving" hit the airwaves in 1964. Recorded by The Four Tops, the song was written and produced by the

Motown team of Holland-Dozier-Holland (Brian Holland, Lamont Dozier and Edward Holland Jr.).

Nothing Like Young Love
The Motown magic of Holland-Dozier-Holland continued on with another hit single in 1964. The Supremes recorded "Baby Love," and the song went on to become one of the group's greatest hits.

Beach Boy Magic

In May 1964, The Beach Boys released "Don't Worry Baby," and if the Internet is any indicator of fan preference, it's considered by some as one of the top 10 Beach Boys lyrics of all time.

Swinging '60s
"Baby I'm Yours" struck the heartstrings of lovers in 1965. The song, written by Van McCoy, was released as a single by Barbara Lewis and hit number 11 on the Billboard Hot 100.

No Smoke and Mirrors

Smokey (William) Robinson wrote several songs with some form of the word "baby" in the title:

- ☛ "Baby, Baby I Need You," recorded by The Temptations in their album *The Temptations Sing Smokey,* released in March 1965

- ☛ "Ooo Baby Baby," written by Smokey and Pete Moore, released by The Miracles in 1965

- ☛ "Baby, Baby Don't Cry," written by Smokey, Al Cleveland and Terry Johnson for The Miracles, released in 1968

- ☛ "Since I Lost My Baby," written by Smokey and Moore, and recorded by The Temptations in 1965

☞ "My Baby Must Be a Magician," recorded by The Marvelettes

☞ "Baby Come Close," released in 1973

☞ "Baby That's Backatcha," recorded during Smokey's solo career in 1975

Who Could Forget You, Babe?

Who could ever forget that wide-eyed, raven-haired beauty who along with her sweetheart belted out the song "I've Got You Babe" for folks in TV land everywhere? The song appeared on Sonny and Cher's first album, *Look at Us,* and hit the number one spot on the singles chart in the summer of 1965. Another of their baby-titled songs also released in 1965, "Baby, Don't Go," did almost as well, hitting number eight on the charts.

Where's the Money?
The Beatles recorded "Baby, You're a Rich Man" in May 1967. It was released in July of that year and was later included on the album *Magical Mystery Tour*. According to Mark Lewisohn, author of *The Complete Beatles Recording Sessions*, it was the first song ever recorded by the Beatles outside of Abbey Road Studios.

Bringing Home the Bread
"Baby I'm-A Want You" was the title single from Bread's fourth album of the same name. It was released in 1972 and topped out at number three on the Billboard Top 100, bringing that group a fair bit of dough, no doubt.

DID YOU  KNOW?

"Baby, Don't Get Hooked on Me" earned singer-songwriter Mac Davis a number one hit in September 1972.

Going in Style
"Rockin' Roll Baby" wasn't a first place finish in 1973, topping out at number 14 on the Billboard Top 100, but it still did well for The Stylistics. In 1975, they released "Thank You Baby." It topped out at number 72.

True Love
Paul Anka and Odia Coates released the single "(You're) Having My Baby" in 1974. Anka wrote the song, which went on to hit number one on the Billboard Hot 100 and remained there from August 24 to September 7, 1974.

One Long Song
The year 1975 was a big one for disco. It was also a big year for Donna Summer—part of the reason for that was her international

disco hit "Love to Love You Baby." Summer first recorded the song as a demo only. Originally, it was released under the name "Love to Love You." But when Summer was persuaded to record a full 16-minute version, complete with (according to *Time* magazine) its 23 orgasmic moans and groans, it was renamed "Love to Love You Baby" and made its way up the Billboard charts, finally landing at number two.

Turning Up the Heat

"Burn Baby Burn," also known as "Disco Inferno," was released by one of the original disco bands, The Trammps. The song came out in 1976 and skyrocketed into hit-single status.

Challenging Copyright

In 1977, Eddie Money released the song "Baby Hold On," and it made it to number 11 on the Billboard Hot 100. There were at least two people, however, who weren't happy with the song's success. Ray Evans and Jay Livingston, writers of the song "Que Sera, Sera (Whatever Will Be, Will Be)," sued Money for plagiarism—they alleged that Money had blended a slightly modified version of two lines from Evans and Livingston's song into his 1977 hit. Money ended up paying damages to the two writers, but it didn't detract from the popularity of "Baby Hold On." If Internet search engines are any indication, the song has a significant following even today.

Their One and Only Baby

In 1977, J.C. Crowley and Peter Beckett of the rock group Player wrote and released the song "Baby Come Back." It made the number one spot on the Billboard Hot 100 in 1978, propelling the band into the public eye and setting the stage for their future success. Although the group continued to record, and individual members successfully worked on independent projects, "Baby Come Back" was Player's only number one hit.

Not So Shocking
"Baby, What a Big Surprise" finished fourth on the Billboard Hot 100 for the group Chicago. It was the first single from the album *Chicago XI,* released in 1977.

Talk the Walk
Dr. Hook showed his quirky side with his song "Baby Makes Her Blue Jeans Talk" in 1982. The song spent 12 weeks at number 25, the highest spot it reached on the Billboard Hot 100 list.

Crossover Hit
In 1991, Christian music artist Amy Grant had her second crossover success with the number one Billboard Hot 100 hit "Baby Baby." Grant explained to the media that she had written the song for her newborn daughter, Millie. She's quoted as saying Millie's "six-week-old face was my inspiration." In 1992, the song was nominated for three Grammy Awards: Song of the Year, Record of the Year, and Best Female Pop Vocal Performance.

Just a Little TLC
"Baby-Baby-Baby" topped out at number two on the Billboard Hot 100 for TLC and hit the top spot on the R&B/Hip Hop charts when the group released it in 1991.

Forever and Always
Mariah Carey hit it big with the song she and rapper Jermaine Dupri co-wrote, "Always Be My Baby." It was released as a single in 1995 and hit the number one spot in the U.S. and number two in Canada, then went on to land on charts around the world.

Just...One More Time

No music hit list is complete without mentioning pop diva Britney Spears, and luckily she did release a song with the word "baby" in the title. "...Baby One More Time" was released in 1999. The popularity of the song, which was the only one on her album to top the Billboard Hot 100, was part of the reason that the debut album of the same name spent 51 weeks floating around the top 10. It also spent an amazing 60 weeks in the top 20 on the U.S. Billboard 200 (a weekly ranking of music albums in the U.S.).

The album gave Britney a giant leap into the industry, and as of the printing of this book, it remains the highest-selling debut album by a female artist in the United States.

Young Virtuoso
Born Percy Romeo Miller Jr. in 1989, he went by the name Lil' Romeo and wasn't much older than a baby himself when his first single, "My Baby," gained the number one spot in 2001. This feat also gave him the distinction of being the youngest artist to earn that honor.

No Doubt a Winner
"Hey Baby" wasn't just a hit song for Gwen Stefani, Tony Kanal, Tom Dumont and Adrian Young of the pop group No Doubt, it also went on to win a Grammy Award in 2003 for Best Pop Performance by a Duo or Group with Vocal.

Dangerously Good
Beyonce's 2003 debut album, *Dangerously in Love*, featured the hit single "Baby Boy." The song, the second released from that album, nestled into the top spot for a full nine weeks.

DID YOU KNOW?

"Baby Girl" was a debut single, and breakthrough recording, for the country music group Sugarland. It was released in 2004 and hit the number two spot on the Billboard Hot Country Singles & Tracks soon thereafter.

Excellent Date

The Red Hot Chili Peppers released "Tell Me Baby" on July 17, 2006—exactly 44 years after I was born, incidentally—and swiftly made it to number one on the Billboard Modern Rock Chart, sitting there for four weeks.

Advertising Flair

In the spring of 2007, the Frankfurt Airport Authority rebranded themselves with flare. That's when they released their theme song, "Baby If We Try We Can Ride Across the Sky." Performed by the Master Session Group, the song is also referred to as the "Song for Frankfurt Airport City."

Baby, Baby, Baby

John Jackson wrote the song "Baby, Don't Go" and released it as a single and on the album *From Nothin' to Somethin'*. It hit the airwaves in 2007.

Double Topping

"Bust It Baby Part 2" topped out at number seven on the Billboard Hot 100 by the summer of 2008 and made it to number two on the R&B/Hip Hop chart. The single was released earlier that year by Plies (featuring Ne-Yo). The song is from Plies' second album, *Definition of Real*, and is the second part of the first single release, "Bust It Baby."

DID YOU KNOW?

It may not be on the Billboard Top 100, but The Jonas Brothers helped make a sweet treat a big hit. They reworked the version of the theme song—which coincidentally, is named after the candy itself—"Baby Bottle Pop." Baby Bottle Pop got its name because the candy is in a baby-bottle-shaped container.

BABY HITS THE BIG SCREEN

We've already established that everyone loves a baby—so much so that the theme has garnered countless hits in the music industry. The story's no different when it comes to the big screen. Even when the plot really has nothing to do with a "baby" per se, movies with the word "baby" in the title have managed to make quite the statement in Hollywood.

Different Kind of Baby

Released in 1933, *Baby Face* caused a lot of controversy in its day. Although the name might suggest the movie has a sweet side, the plot is actually edgy and sexually charged. Barbara Stanwyck, starring in the leading role of Lily Powers (a.k.a. Baby Face), "climbed the ladder of success—wrong by wrong," as the movie's tagline says.

Baby-Faced Starlet

The musical comedy *Baby Take a Bow* hit theaters in 1934. Based on the James Judge play *Square Crooks*, the "baby" in the story is a young Shirley Temple who's faced with getting her ex-con father out of a frame-up.

One Sweet Kitty

Katherine Hepburn starred in the 1938 movie *Bringing Up Baby*. The "baby" in this comedy is actually a leopard.

Comic Strip Baby

Blondie 4: Blondie Brings Up a Baby is, kind of, about a baby. The fourth in the series of five movies based on Chic Young's comic strip *Blondie* was released in 1939 and starred Penny

Singleton as the lead female character, Blondie. The "baby" in this film is Blondie and Dagwood's son, Alexander, a.k.a. Baby Dumpling.

Eight in the House

Jerry Lewis stars opposite Carla Naples (Marilyn Maxwell) in the leading role in the 1958 comedy *Rock-a-Bye Baby*. In this instance, the movie title certainly isn't misleading. Lewis, playing TV repairman Clayton Poole, agrees to take care of his high-school-sweetheart-turned-actress' baby triplets to help her avoid a Hollywood scandal. But in order to adopt the babies, he has to be married, so he marries Carla's sister Sandy. Nine months later, Lewis becomes a daddy to his original trio, plus five more, leaving no shortage of babies in this comedy.

DID YOU KNOW?

Jack Nicholson made his film debut in the 1958 movie *The Cry Baby Killer*. Starring as the teenaged delinquent Jimmy Wallace, he finds himself overwhelmed at the thought that he may have killed someone, hence the moniker "Cry Baby."

When Baby Grows Up

Bette Davis and Joan Crawford starred as the Hollywood sisters Jane and Blanche Hudson in the 1962 film *Whatever Happened to Baby Jane?* Of course, Jane Hudson was once "baby Jane," and the plot deals with the twists and turns of fate that life leads the sisters through.

The Darker Side

The title of the 1964 black-comedy film *Spider Baby* doesn't leave a lot of room for doubt as to the genre of this flick. Starring Lon Chaney Jr., the movie is about three mentally, socially and physically challenged children, one of whom is nicknamed "Spider Baby" because of her spider-like movements.

More About the Rain

There are no babies in the 1965 movie *Baby the Rain Must Fall*. Steve McQueen stars as an ex-con, and Lee Remmick stars as his wife in this relationship drama that lives up to its tagline: "The more he gets into trouble, the more he gets under her skin!"

Saying Goodbye to Marital Bliss

Talk about domestic tension! Husband and wife duo Nick Johnson (played by Tony Curtis) and Francesca (Rosanna Schiaffino) face off against each other in the 1966 movie *Arrivederci, Baby!*

When Baby Grows Up!

The 1967 film *Carmen, Baby* is another story referring to an altogether different sort of baby. Uta Levka was cast in the role of Carmen, a hip and modern variation on the classical *Carmen*.

That's Just Nasty

Kill Baby Kill, an Italian movie released in 1968, starred Giacomo Rossi-Stuart and Erika Blanc and is a dark, gothic, horror flick. Nothing at all to do with babies here!

Disturbing Twist

The Roman Polanski film *Rosemary's Baby* was another psychological thriller/horror movie released in 1968. The movie, based on the book of the same name by Ira Levin, starred Mia Farrow and John Cassavetes.

When You Need a Little Help

There's no doubt about the literal meaning behind this movie's title. Barbara Hershey played the leading-lady role of Tish Gray, a young woman hired as a surrogate mother, in the 1970 film *Baby Maker*.

A Moniker with Meaning

Bizarre is just one of the many adjectives used by reviewers to describe the 1972 movie *The Baby*. Far from being a happy little flick, this horror film has Anjanette Comer starring in the role of social worker Ann Gentry. Gentry squares off against a Mrs. Wadsworth (Ruth Roman) and her daughters in a battle to have the family's adult son—nicknamed "Baby" because of his significantly immature mental age—placed in care, away from his seemingly abusive family.

Babies, Manga Style

The *Lone Wolf and Cub* manga (Japanese comic) series, written by Kazuo Koike and illustrated by Goseki Kojima, has spawned several television series and full-length feature films. Among them is the 1972 release *Lone Wolf and Cub: Baby Cart at the River Styx*, as well as the 1974 release *Lone Wolf and Cub: Baby Cart to Hades*. Both films starred Tomisaburo Wakayama in the lead character role of Ogami Itto. The "cub" in the equation is Itto's son, Daigoro, who accompanies his assassin father on his journeys.

DID YOU KNOW?

The 1973 movie *Trick Baby* contains a lot more than just a mischievous youngster. The action crime drama, based on the novel of the same name by Robert Beck, merits its tagline: "Sometimes even the players get played."

Tagline Disclaimer

Sheba, Baby, the 1975 release starring Pam Grier, is another baby-named movie you should think twice about before you turn it on in front of the little ones. Grier plays the role of

Sheba, and this action thriller touts itself as being "Hotter 'n 'Coffy,' Meaner 'n 'Foxy Brown.'"

Keeping Baby Safe

The title of this 1977 made-for-TV movie pretty much gives away the plot—and in this case a baby, or a soon-to-be baby, is involved. *Black Market Baby* stars a young Linda Purl and Desi Arnaz Jr. playing a couple who are expecting a baby and are targeted by an underground adoption ring.

Pretty Protégé

The 1978 debut movie for Brooke Shields was about as full of controversy as the story's content. *Pretty Baby*, described as a "historical drama," dealt with the touchy subject of child prostitution. The 12-year-old Shields—who, if you haven't yet guessed, is the "Pretty Baby" of the film—was photographed naked, posing naughtily for a traveling photographer who happens by her mother's "establishment."

Where's the Baby?

It seems that horror films have a knack for tossing their viewers a few red herrings, at least as far as their titles go. *Manhattan Baby* is another baby-titled horror flick. This one is Italian in origin and was released in 1982. It also went by several other names—*L'Occhio del male, Eye of the Evil Dead, Evil Eye* and *The Possessed*—any of which would have been eminently less deceiving.

Baby in a Big Way

The 1985 film *Baby: Secret of the Lost Legend* is, surprising as it might seem by now, actually about a baby...of sorts. The "baby" in question is a tiny brontosaurus who, along with his family, is discovered by an American couple traveling through Central

Africa. Strangely enough, the movie is based on an African legend about such creatures actually roaming the area.

Where's My Mama?

Probably the easiest recognizable baby-themed movie in the last few decades starred Tom Selleck, Steve Guttenberg and Ted Danson posing as three carefree bachelors who suddenly find themselves caring for a baby who was supposedly fathered by one of them. The film *3 Men and a Baby* hit theaters in 1987, and although the young, hot bachelors weren't ready for what was about to unfold, the audience couldn't wait for it. As the baby in the movie grew, so too did the men caring for her. The sequel entitled *3 Men and a Little Lady* was released in 1990, bringing a bit of closure to this quirky love story.

From Big Screen to TV
Diane Keaton starred as career woman J.C. Wiatt in the 1987 comedy *Baby Boom*. In the middle of her busy lifestyle Wiatt finds herself parenting the toddler of a distant relative who dies suddenly. Baby, of course, has Wiatt not only juggling responsibilities but priorities as well. The movie did so well that it spawned a television series, which ran for two seasons in 1988 and 1989.

We're Pregnant?
Kevin Bacon and Elizabeth McGovern starred as Jake and Kristy Briggs in the 1988 release *She's Having a Baby*. The movie deals with the stresses of new parenthood and the temptations that, if we're honest, we all feel from time to time.

DID YOU KNOW?

Parenthood, starring Steve Martin as the somewhat bumbling father of two, is another Hollywood film that spurred the production of a television series. The movie hit theaters in 1989, and the television series started running in 1990.

Once, Twice, Three Times a Hit
The romantic comedy *Look Who's Talking* was so successful when it appeared on the big screen in 1989 that it spawned the sequel *Look Who's Talking Too* a year later and *Look Who's Talking Now* in 1993. Babies were the big hit in the first two movies, giving the adult world a glimpse into what the little gaffers might be thinking from time to time. In the third incarnation, the family pets also get a voice.

It's All About the Countdown

The romantic comedy *Nine Months* was released in the summer of 1995. As the tagline suggests, "ready or not," someone's pregnant—and Samuel Faulkner (Hugh Grant) and Rebecca Taylor (Julianne Moore) have more than the usual adjustments to make before the big day.

Who's the Daddy?

The Object of My Affection, released in 1998, puts a little twist on what a family looks like. This movie features a pregnant Nina Borowski (Jennifer Aniston), the would-be father George Hanson (Paul Rudd) and, just for good measure, Nina's best—and gay—friend Vince McBride (John Pankow). The man who ends up playing daddy to the baby-to-be is the mystery in this comedy.

Smarter Than I Look

As the tagline suggests, "Naps are history" in *Baby Geniuses*. In this 1999 crime comedy, a crooked scientist holds baby geniuses captive.

Bringing Home Baby

Getting to know your in-laws is a piece of cake. The tough part really starts when the babies come along. This is the subject of the 1995 comedy *Father of the Bride Part II*.

Lost, Abducted

The 2007 movie *Gone Baby Gone* is a crime drama focused on the abduction of a four-year-old girl and, later, a seven-year-old boy. The movie stars Casey Affleck, Michelle Monaghan and Morgan Freeman.

NIGHTTIME RITUALS

*Bedtime is sometimes the best time of day. A warm, sudsy
bath. Milk and a cookie. A warm quilt. A cuddle with
Mama or Papa. And all that remains is a cupboard full of
nursery rhymes and stories. Here are a few of the favorites
collected throughout the years. The authors of many of these
verses, as well as any concrete information on when they
were written, are lost to history. But the verses—although
there are often several versions of each—have survived,
allowing parents to lull their children to sleep through
the ages.*

The Big Day

In most cultures in the world, a great deal of significance is
attached to the day you were born. The following poem has
appeared in numerous renditions, though this version is believed
to be the original, composed in 1887 as part of a serialized fic-
tion story appearing in the September 17 issue of the American
publication *Harper's Weekly*:

Monday's child is fair of face.
Tuesday's child is full of grace.
Wednesday's child is loving and giving.
Thursday's child works hard for a living.
Friday's child is full of woe.
Saturday's child has far to go.
But the child that is born on the Sabbath-day
Is bonny and happy and wise and gay.

(Many of you will jump on me and say I've got it all wrong.
That's because you're thinking of the version we're all familiar
with, in which Wednesday's child who "is full of woe," and
Thursday's child "has far to go.")

"Sleep, Baby, Sleep!"

The author of this rhyme is unknown, though, truth be told, there must be several authors because there are several versions and various numbers of stanzas of the rhyme.

Sleep, baby, sleep!
Thy father guards the sheep.
Thy mother shakes the dreamland tree,
And from it fall sweet dreams for thee,
Sleep, baby, sleep.

"Rock-a-Bye (Hush-a-bye) Baby"

This is one of those nursery rhymes that leave you scratching your head in wonder. Think about it: baby is placed in a cradle, up high, and rocked until he falls to the ground. Kind of grim if you ask me. Someone, somewhere, must have had one tough night with their little one to come up with these words—or at least you would think. However, there are a few explanations behind the origin of this rhyme, and none of them sound like Mama was stressed.

One story dates back to England in the 1700s. In the tale, the Kenyons, a family of charcoal burners, lived in the woods near the Betty Kenny Tree, a yew tree thought to be 2000 years old and named after mother (Kate) Kenyon. With eight children, you have to get inventive when it comes to sleeping arrangements, and so one of the tree's boughs was carved into a cradle. There is some suggestion the rhyme relates to the Kenyon family.

Another story behind the rhyme dates the verse back to the Glorious Revolution, otherwise known as the Revolution of 1688. If you need a refresher on British history, that's when William of Orange and his army overthrew King James II and became King William III of England. The theory goes that the baby represents King James II (who was rumored in some circles to be an impostor anyway); the blowing wind represents the wind of change in the political scene of the day; and the monarchy is represented by the cradle. While the last suggested origin of the verse might make the violent aspects of the rhyme a little more understandable, it does seem a little far-fetched. But don't despair. There is yet another suggestion to consider.

According to the *Great American Baby Almanac,* another legend credits the verse to an American pilgrim boy fresh off the *Mayflower.* The story goes that the boy wrote the verse after

watching Native American mothers place their babies in birchbark cradles suspended from tree branches. The cradles rocked gently in the breeze, lulling baby to sleep.

It doesn't really matter which story is true, although both renditions provide answers to those obvious questions we've all had. And the first verse of the beloved rhyme is something just about everyone in the Western world can recite. Modern versions of the lullaby often have additional verses, and the authors of those verses are usually known.

Rock-a-bye baby, on the treetop
When the wind blows, the cradle will rock
When the bough breaks, the cradle will fall
And down will come baby, cradle and all

"Mockingbird Song (Hush, Little Baby)"

There doesn't appear to be much information on this little ditty, including a credit for whoever authored the piece. However, despite its indulgent verses, it has an air of truth to it, don't you think? After all, what daddy doesn't love to spoil his girl?

Hush little baby, don't say a word,
Papa's going to buy you a mockingbird.
If that mockingbird won't sing,
Papa's going to buy you a diamond ring.
If that diamond ring turns brass,
Papa's going to buy you a looking glass.
If that looking glass gets broke,
Papa's going to buy you a billy goat.
If that billy goat won't pull,
Papa's going to buy you a cart and bull.
If that cart and bull fall down,
You'll still be the sweetest little baby in town.

MAKING THE BED

So you or someone you know is expecting a baby.
Congratulations! Of course, you do realize this means
you have to prepare a whole lot of things before baby comes.
While there are many items you need to obtain—from
clothing and feeding supplies to diapering and bathing
supplies—one of the biggest, all-encompassing preparations
you'll ever make is designing baby's nursery. If you know
the baby's sex, perhaps you've chosen the standard pink
or blue. Or maybe you want to be surprised, so you've
decided to go with a neutral yellow and green in order

*to cater to either sex. Or maybe you've got bold colors
in your plans—that artistic flair will get you brownie
points for originality, and you'll have a lot of fun putting
something together that no other baby has.*

*Baby's room is a little piece of heaven for your newborn.
Why not give the space a personal touch that says
something about who your family is, what you stand for and
what you hope to instill into your child?*

Tried and True

You can't throw a stuffed bear in the baby section without coming across something with a Winnie the Pooh theme on it. For as long as I can remember, the "bear of very little brain" has been all the rage when it comes to generic or boy-themed nurseries, and he's become even more popular of late. You can get Winnie the Pooh glasses, blankets, bedding, towels, toothbrushes, memory books, photo albums…is there no end?

Classical Elegance
If you know you're having a girl, and you're a fan of the novel *The Secret Garden*, there are stores that create beautiful sets of bedding themed after the story.

An Early Education

Looking for something unisex? How about an alphabet-themed room? It's something that won't get tired for several years after baby is born—or at least until your little genius has learned the alphabet. And somehow, whenever I think of the alphabet, I think of bold primary colors—might as well get on with those lessons early!

Lions and Tigers and Bears...

Another unisex idea is going with an animal theme. And if you're inclined to argue that animals aren't feminine enough for a little girl, think again. Little Bindy Irwin, daughter of the late Steve Irwin and a wildlife conservation activist in her own right, would most likely disagree. According to the statement she read at her father's memorial service, this young woman is a diehard wildlife enthusiast—something she hopes others will eventually relate to. And if you're wondering, there is no limit to the wallpaper and bedding options out there related to this subject.

Environmentally Aware

Then there's the rain forest theme. Not to be confused with a generic animal theme, designing your baby's room around the idea of a rain forest is another idea that gives you countless options. There are a whole lot of accessories and color themes that would blend well with the traditional baby bedding and accessories. Many stores that provide baby products sell mobiles, wall hangings, wallpaper borders and even toys. You could also go wild, as it were, by free-styling the walls with your own interpretation of what a rainforest looks like. Yes! Why not try painting a mural? Use bold greens, reds and blues for bedding and accessories, and your little one will have a one-of-a-kind sleeping palace.

Heritage Themes

If personalizing your nursery is important, consider decorating it in a way that shows off some of your family's personality. For example, if you're a farmer, find a wallpaper border that reflects that. Visit your local farm dealership and purchase a few collectable, die-cast toy tractors. And have Grandma make a quilt with a farm scene on it. You get the idea.

Going the Traditional Route

If you know the sex of your child, and you're a traditionalist, you could play off the old rhyme outlining what little girls and boys are made of. When it comes to girls, "sugar and spice and all things nice," the possibilities are seemingly limitless. Pink and pretty sums it up. But consider working with what little boys are made of: "snips and snails and puppy dog tails." *That* might take a little more effort—and might produce a very interesting room!

Biblical Narrative

Noah's Ark is the obvious choice when it comes to planning for a Biblical theme for your newborn. Noah's Ark bedding and mobiles and bumper pads can be found at just about every retail outlet. But if you're looking for something a little different, why not create a Garden of Eden—a twist on the rain forest theme. Go ahead. I bet you can think of a dozen other good ideas!

Baby-Inspired Art

Anyone who has ever walked down the picture aisle of any large department store or browsed through the photography section of a bookstore has likely seen the work of Australian-born baby photographer extraordinaire Anne Geddes. The babies she photographs are almost fairy-like, their images tied to the natural world in some way. Geddes usually adorns the babies in ornate costumes representing flowers, bees, butterflies or bunnies, to name a few. The babies are frequently photographed gazing about peacefully. Sometimes they're sleeping. Sometimes two or more are looking at one another. And although the scenes are all very different, their surreal nature ties them together, and you immediately recognize the famed photographer's work.

In the Palm of Her Hand

The work of British Columbia artist Camille Allen is so one-of-a-kind that it echoes her name as soon as you see it. Allen, an artist who has spent the last five years focusing on more traditional-sized dolls and sculptures, has developed a unique way to use up small portions of polymer clay leftover from these larger projects. She's taken to carving babies so small you can hold them in the palm of your hand or put them inside an egg. As if these creations weren't lifelike enough, Allen applies mohair and paint to enhance the wrinkles and give the baby's "skin" a soft, downy feel.

Allen, who's just 27 years old and has been busy building her artistic repertoire, will no doubt make a worldwide name for herself—she's already made it into the 2008 edition of *Ripley's Believe It or Not*.

INTERESTING CELEBRITY BABY NAMES

As a journalism student working an internship at a small community newspaper almost two decades ago, I came across a birth announcement welcoming a baby girl into a well-known farming family in the area. It was August, and the baby—who was born in the wee hours of the morning—was named Summer Dawn. By then I'd birthed and named four children, and at the time I wasn't planning to add to that brood, but I couldn't help but think that should I have another child, I'd have liked to break loose of my somewhat conservative nature and pick a name that stands out.

Of course, there can be downfalls to such an adventure. Kids can be cruel. But I think Johnny Cash sang it best in his famous song about a boy named Sue. Having an unusual name builds character. If folks like you and I choose interesting names for our children, they aren't usually recognized in a big way. Celebrities, on the other hand, are a little different. When they choose an interesting name for their offspring, the whole world gets to hear about it!

The Zappa Family

Perhaps the most famous unusual celebrity baby names belong to the four children of the Zappa family. Moon Unit (September 28, 1967), Dweezil (September 5, 1968), Ahmet Emuukha Rodan (May 15, 1974) and Diva Thin Muffin Pigeen (July 30, 1979) were born to famed rocker Frank Zappa and his second wife, Adelaide Gail Sloatman. The unusual naming, however, is just part of the story.

The family's first child, Moon Unit, goes by the name of Moon Zappa, saying "Unit" is her middle name. Their second child has always gone by the name Dweezil. However, one source told the story of how hospital authorities at the time wouldn't allow the new baby to be registered by that name, so the name that appeared on his original birth certificate was Ian Donald Calvin Euclid Zappa. These were the first names of four of Zappa's friends and were thought up on the spur of the moment to satisfy the nurse taking down the information. At the age of five, Dweezil discovered these names on his birth certificate and wanted it changed. It took a lawyer to do it, but his birth certificate now reads "Dweezil."

On an interesting side note, the name Dweezil was originally the "technical name" Frank gave one of Gail's toes. According to *The Real Frank Zappa Book*, Frank explains this "funny looking toe…had been the source of family amusement so often that it acquired a 'technical name': it wasn't really a toe—it was a 'Dweezil.' I thought then and continue to think today, that Dweezil is a nice name."

Just how baby number three acquired his name isn't quite as dramatic as his older brother. Ahmet was named after one of the founding brothers of Atlantic Records, Ahmet Ertegun. With regard to his last child, in a 1982 interview Frank explained that his youngest got her name Diva because "she was screaming louder than all the other babies in the nursery."

It appears the love for unique names has continued on down the family chain. Moon and rock star hubby Paul Doucette, of Matchbox Twenty fame, welcomed daughter Mathilda Plum into the world on December 21, 2004. Dweezil and wife Lauren Knudsen welcomed their firstborn in 2006. The couple named their baby girl Zola Frank Zappa.

Holy Crime Fighter!

Perhaps it's only natural that Penn Jillette, of the Las Vegas comedy and illusion act Penn & Teller, has a penchant for unique names. His own name, after all, isn't incredibly common. (By the way, Penn is a name of English origin meaning "lives by the hill.") Penn and wife Emily Zolten chose Moxie CrimeFighter as the name for their daughter, born on June 3, 2005, and Zolten Penn for their son born May 22, 2006.

Soft and Sweet

British television personality Jonathan Ross and his wife, journalist and author Jane Goldman, have birthed two children with interesting names: Betty Kitten and Honey Kinny. Their middle child and only son has the more conventional name of Harvey Kirby.

In the Middle
Tommy Lee Jones and his second wife, Kimberlea Cloughley, chose Kafka as the middle name of their first child, daughter Victoria, born in 1991.

DID YOU KNOW?

Spice Girl Mel-B and first husband Jimmy Gulzar named the baby girl they had together Phoenix Chi (born February 19, 1999). "Phoenix" is Greek in origin and means "blood red," while "Chi" is of Chinese origin and means "younger energy."

Unique Combination
Randy Jackson, of The Jackson 5 fame, and Eliza Shaffe have one daughter together, Stevanna, born June 17, 1990. The name Stevanna is an American twist on the names Steve and Anna.

Making a Statement

Speaking of the Jacksons, Michael Jackson is father to three children, two of which are named Prince Michael I (a.k.a. Prince) and Prince Michael II (a.k.a. Blanket).

Salute to the Sea

American model Christie Brinkley and fourth husband Peter Cook chose an interesting name for the couple's first, and Christie's third, child. They named their daughter, born on July 2, 1998, Sailor Lee.

Long and Graceful

Actors Jada Pinkett Smith and husband Will Smith named their second child, born on October 31, 2000, Willow. The English name comes from the willow tree.

Looking to the Stars

Actor and business owner Chris Noth and his girlfriend, Canadian actress Tara Wilson, welcomed baby boy Orion into the world on January 18, 2008. The name is Greek in origin and means "dweller on the mountain." For those of you not up on Greek myths, Orion was the name of a mythological hunter.

Wholesome Goodness

Actress Gwyneth Paltrow and British rock star Chris Martin chose a fragrant and sweet name for their baby girl Apple, who

was born on May 14, 2004. When asked about the unusual name when she appeared on *Oprah*, Paltrow said, "It sounded so sweet and it conjured such a lovely picture for me. You know, apples are so sweet and they're wholesome and it's Biblical and I just thought it sounded so lovely and clean! And I just thought, 'Perfect!'" A second child, born on April 8, 2006, was named Moses, another name with a strong Biblical connection.

Water Baby
Actress Keri Russell and carpenter hubby Shane Deary welcomed their first child, baby boy River, into the world on June 9, 2007. The name is English in origin.

Who Doesn't Love Chocolate?

Actors Courteney Cox and David Arquette named their first child Coco. The bouncing baby girl was born on June 13, 2004, just a day after the couple's fifth wedding anniversary and a couple of days before Courteney turned 40. Incidentally, "Coco" is listed on the Internet Movie Database as one of Courteney's nicknames.

Religious Significance

Baby boy Cruz is a third son for Victoria (Spice Girls fame) and David Beckham (soccer superstar), born February 20, 2005. Cruz is pronounced "Cruth," which means "the cross of Christ," and is of Spanish origin.

Z-O-W-I-E!

Singer David Bowie and his first wife Angela gave their son a catchy name no one will ever forget—Zowie. Born on May 30, 1971, Zowie chooses to go by his legal birth name, Duncan Zowie Haywood Jones.

The Most Unique of All

Rock and roll legend James Brown fathered several sons and daughters throughout his four marriages, but his daughter Yamma Noyola (now Dr. Yamma Noyola Brown Lumar) wins out as having the most unique name of the bunch.

Resurrected Favorite

Actor David Baldwin and his second wife Isabella Hofmann welcomed baby boy Atticus into the world on July 13, 1996. It's believed that they named their son after the lawyer character in *To Kill a Mockingbird*.

DID YOU KNOW?

Singer Ashley Ward Parker and his fiancée Tiffany Lynn chose the name Lyric for their son, who was born in August 2005.

Say It with Meaning

Actors Michael J. Fox and his wife Tracy Pollan have a knack for choosing interesting names for their youngsters. Twins

Aquinnah (Native American for "high land") and Schuyler (Dutch for "scholar") were born on February 15, 1995. Baby Esmé (French for "loved") came along a few years later, on November 3, 2001. Son Samuel is the couple's oldest, born May 30, 1989, and although he has a more traditional name, I couldn't just leave him out of the spotlight altogether.

Names with Flavor
Chef and Food Network personality Jamie Oliver and his wife Juliette Norton named their girls Poppy Honey (March 18, 2002) and Daisy Boo (April 11, 2003).

Super Name

Actor Nicholas Cage and his wife Alice Kim named their son, born October 3, 2005, Kal-El. The name is also Superman's Kryptonian name.

Musical Flair
Australian actress Rachel Griffiths and artist Andrew Taylor named their first child, born November 22, 2003, Banjo Patrick.

Many Meanings
American actress Gillian Leigh Anderson (best known for her role as Agent Dana Scully of *The X-Files*) and first husband Clyde Klotz, an art director with the TV show, named their daughter Piper Maru. "Piper" is of English origin, meaning "flute player," and "Maru" is typically a boy's name originating from the Pacific Islands and refers to the Moriori god of healing. One of *The X-Files* episodes was named after the little girl.

Honoring Grandpa

Singer John Mellencamp and his third wife Elaine Irwin gave their second son a name that had folks talking for some time after his birth. Speck Wildhorse was born in 1995. "Speck" was

John's grandfather's name, and one can only assume choosing "Wildhorse" has to do with father-like-son. After all, John's middle name is Cougar.

Heaven Blessed
On November 26, 2000, actress Nia Long and her fiancé at the time, actor Massai Dorsey, welcomed son Massai Zhivago Dorsey II into the world. Massai (also spelled Masai) is a Hebrew name meaning "God's work." Zhivago is a Russian name meaning "daring."

Starlight, Star Bright

Actress and model Marissa Berenson and her first husband James Randall had one daughter together. Starlite Melody was born in 1977.

Give Me Some Love
R&B singer and songwriter Lil' Mo (a.k.a. Cynthia Loving) and one-time husband Al Stone had two daughters whose names reflect their mother's birth name: Heaven Love'on Stone (August 19, 2002) and God'Iss Love Stone (February 24, 2005).

Five Fine Names

Arlyn Phoenix, a political activist also known as Heart Phoenix, had five children. All have interesting names and all are no stranger to the bright lights of Hollywood: River Jude (b. August 23, 1970; d. October 31, 1993), Rain Joan of Arc (March 31, 1973), Joaquin Rafael Phoenix (October 28, 1974), Liberty Mariposa (July 5, 1976) and Summer Joy (December 10, 1978).

Techno Bound?
Shannyn Sossamon, American actress and all-round performer, has one child with Dallas Clayton. Their son, Audio Science, was born on May 29, 2003.

The name Mateo is the Spanish form of the name Matthew, which means "gift of God." It was the name actors Benjamin Bratt and his wife Talisa Soto chose for their son, who was born on October 3, 2005.

Beyond Unique

During the union between Boomtown Rats lead singer Bob Geldof and British television personality Paula Elizabeth Yates, three lovely daughters were born: Fifi Trixibelle Geldof (March 31, 1983), Peaches Honeyblossom Michelle Charlotte Angel Vanessa Geldof (March 16, 1989) and Pixie Geldof (September 17, 1990). Following the couple's divorce, Paula partnered with INXS singer Michael Hutchence and had another daughter, Heavenly Hiraani Tiger Lily Hutchence, who was born July 22, 1996.

Going All Out

British folk rocker Donovan (Donovan Phillips Leitch) had a knack for choosing interesting names for his youngsters. The first of two children born to partner Enid Karl Stulberger was named after himself (Donovan junior was born August 16, 1968), but daughter Ione Skye started the unique naming tradition going. The name "Ione" is of Greek origin and means "of Ionia." Daughters Astrella Celeste and Oriole Nebula came along after Donovan split with Enid and married Linda Lawrence. "Astrella" is of English origin and means "star." "Oriole" is of Latin origin and refers to the oriole bird.

Family Tree

Actor Nick Nolte and his third wife Rebecca Linger named their son, born June 20, 1986, a good, strong Irish name, Brawley. It means "descendant of Brolach."

Simple Strength

Actor Forest Whitaker has four children with interesting names. His son Ocean Alexander was born to Forest and then-partner Raye Dowell in 1990. In 1996 Forest and Keisha Nash married, and the pair welcomed Sonnet Noel (born October 3, 1996) and True Isabella Summer (born July 2, 1998) into the family. Keisha also has a daughter named Autumn (born in 1991) from a previous relationship.

Precious Horses

The marriage between American film producer and director Steven Spielberg and his second wife, Kate Capshaw, produced a daughter, born December 1, 1996, with a memorable if unusual name—Destry Allyn. "Destry" is American in origin and means "horse keeper," while "Allyn" is a variation of the name Alan or Allen, an Old German name meaning "precious."

Name Change

Hollywood icon Woody Allen has had his fair share of children from a couple of relationships. Satchel Farrow (who now goes by the name Ronan Seamus Farrow) was born on December 19, 1987, to Allen and actress Mia Farrow during their 12-year relationship. Their marriage dissolved after a highly publicized relationship between Allen and Farrow's adopted daughter Soon-Yi was revealed in 1992. Allen and Soon-Yi married five years later and adopted two girls, whom they named Bechet Dumaine and Manzie Tio. Both girls are named after jazz musicians—Sidney Bechet and Manzie Johnson, a drummer in Bechet's band.

Abundant Love

Actress Helen Hunt and partner Matthew Carnahan welcomed daughter Makena Lei into their world on May 13, 2004. "Makena" is a unisex name of Hawaiian origin. It means "abundance."

DID YOU KNOW?

Two-time World Heavyweight Boxing Champion George Foreman has 10 children from three different marriages. All five boys are named—you guessed it—George, numbers I to V. George also has five daughters, two of whom bear a rendition of the name George: Freeda George and Georgetta.

What the People Think

In 2004, Sky Digital's Family Active service conducted a survey of 1000 Britons. Their goal was to uncover what folks there believed were the 20 strangest celebrity names. While "Moon Unit" took first place hands down, and names such as "Fifi Trixibelle" and "Apple" were also on the list, there were a few surprises. Most notably was the inclusion of a member of Britain's Royal Family. It seems Brits think Eugenie, daughter of Sarah Ferguson and Prince Andrew, deserves a significant placing. It ranked as the 15th oddest name. The name is of French origin and means "well born," which if you think about it, suits the royal daughter just fine.

MAKING YOUR MARK EARLY IN LIFE

*Shakespeare, the ultimate wordsmith of all time, wrote
in the play* Twelfth Night, *"Some are born great, some
achieve greatness, and others have greatness thrust upon
them." It appears, at least when it comes to famous babies
throughout history, being born into greatness or having
it thrust upon you are the most likely options. Poor little
munchkins. Didn't know it was coming!*

And They Said It Couldn't Be Done

Thomas Beatie made worldwide headlines when he became the
first man in history to become pregnant and give birth. Thirty-
four-year-old Thomas was born a female but never felt right in
his own skin. He met his wife Nancy while still a woman, and
Nancy supported him every step of the way to becoming a
transgender male. The couple married, and on June 28, 2008,
welcomed 9-pound, 5-ounce, 21¾-inch Susan Juliette Beatie
into the world, making this little darling—and her famous
father—the most talked about father-daughter duo around.

Nancy certainly isn't to be left out of the equation. Although she
wasn't able to conceive a child, she took hormones and used a
breast pump to prepare her body to breastfeed the couple's baby.
Thomas had kept some of his female organs thinking they would
want to have a child, knowing that would have to be his role, and
when the couple was ready, he underwent in vitro fertilization.
However, Thomas insists he's daddy, not mommy, and when
Susan starts crying for dinner, he's more than happy to have
Nancy step in. So for every pregnant woman who has ever wished
that her male partner could understand for a moment what she
was going through, this story is something to think about.

Drawn from the Water

Ask an Old Testament scholar to name the most famous baby in that portion of the Bible, and he'll likely mention Moses. The Hebrew name, which apparently means "savior" and "drawn from the water," was given to the son of a Hebrew mother named Jochebed after the Pharaoh issued a decree to kill all newborn boys of Hebrew descent. Jochebed placed her son in a basket and asked her daughter, Miriam, to float the basket in the Nile River, near where the Pharaoh's daughter Thermuthis (or Bithiah) was sure to spot him. Thermuthis did indeed find the basket and took in the baby boy as her own. Miriam, a nosy sister looking to ensure the well-being of her baby brother, was lurking nearby and approached Thermuthis, discretely suggesting that she knew of a Hebrew woman who'd recently lost her baby and could nurse this newborn. Jochebed was then able to resume her place with her son, though as his nurse and not his mother. When he became an adult, and his true heritage was revealed to him, Moses went on to lead his people out of slavery and into the land of Canaan.

Christmas Babe

The New Testament's famous baby was, of course, Jesus Christ. According to Christian teaching, the Old Testament prophets foretold his birth, calling him the Messiah or Son of God and telling of how he'd deliver Israel from the oppression and bondage imposed by the ruling powers of the day. In a sense, Christ's resurrection from the dead after being crucified on the cross symbolized another type of birth—a birth after death that was offered to those who believed in his teachings.

Of Aviation Fame

Charles Lindbergh was already a famous aviator from a well-known family when he was thrust into the public spotlight in a big way in the evening hours of March 1, 1932. That's when

Betty Gow, the family's nurse, discovered Charles Junior missing from his nursery. The New Jersey State Police were called immediately, and from the evidence gathered at the scene, it was determined that the 20-month-old had been kidnapped for ransom money. The money was eventually delivered at a predetermined location, but the baby was never returned. Two years later, detectives gathered enough evidence to arrest Bruno Hauptmann. He was later tried and found guilty of kidnapping and murder, although the body of baby Charles was never discovered.

Madonna Mania

Rock star diva Madonna has had her share of the press, but perhaps one of her most controversial bouts in the public eye occurred shortly after she announced she would adopt David Banda, a baby from Malawi. Madonna and her husband Guy Ritchie planned their adoption of the little boy after reportedly receiving the blessing of David's birth father. Baby David's mother died shortly after his birth, and the boy lived in an orphanage until he was a year old. At that time, Madonna and Ritchie took interim custody of the boy for 18 months until the Malawi government finalized the adoption.

Young Leaders

The Tibetan Buddhist practice of recognizing their spiritual leader the Dalai Lama at a very young age—many of them barely out of infancy—dates back to their earliest recorded history. Lobsang Gyatso was recognized as the fifth Dalai Lama in 1618, at just a year old. Tsangyang Gyatso followed him in 1688 at the age of five. The eighth Dalai Lama, Jamphel Gyatso, was two, and Lungtok Gyatso followed him when he was a year old. Tsultrim Gyatso was four when he became the 10th incarnation; Khendrup Gyatso was two when he took the title of the 11th Dalai Lama; Trinley Gyatso was three on becoming the 12th

Dalai Lama; Thubten Gyatso was two when he took the 13th incarnation; and the current and 14th Dalai Lama, Tenzin Gyatso, was four when he was first recognized. With this kind of recorded history, it's quite likely the unmentioned incarnations were also very young when they received their titles. That's a whole lot of famous babies!

DID YOU KNOW?

Apparently Baby New Year, the personification of the New Year as a baby wearing little more than a diaper and sash, is a custom that comes from Greece, originating as far back as 600 BC. It appears the Greeks celebrated the rebirth of Dionysus, the god of wine, every New Year. The Egyptians also use a baby to symbolize the rebirth of the New Year.

Happy New Year, Birthday Baby!

Every New Year in modern history, communities worldwide have recognized the first baby born on that day. Likely the tradition has something to do with the symbolic connection of new birth and the birth of a New Year. Whatever the reason, there have been some pretty interesting names associated with the title of New Year's baby:

☞ Pope Alexander VI made his grand entry into the world in 1431. He was 61 when he became what was later described by one source as "the most controversial of the secular popes of the Renaissance."

☞ The first Director of the Federal Bureau of Investigation in the United States, J. Edgar Hoover, was born on New Year's Day in 1895.

☞ Anyone who loves to read and takes an interest in modern literature likely knows of the novel *The Catcher in the Rye* and its author J.D. Salinger. He entered the world on January 1, 1919.

☞ Kala Sosefina Mileniume Kauvaka, a little girl with a very impressive handle, was born in the city of Nuku'Alofa, Tonga, at 12:06 AM in the year 2000, giving her universal recognition as the first baby to be born in the new millennium.

A LOOK AT NATURE'S BABIES

Let's face it. We share this wonderful world with a plethora of other species, and a book on baby trivia would be sadly lacking if it didn't share a few of their oddities as well. Check it out!

A Whale of a Story

It's no surprise that nature's largest animal can produce a whale of an offspring. The blue whale, for example, makes its grand entry into the world measuring about 25 feet in length and weighing in at a whopping six to eight tons. It's no wonder the youngster has an appetite large enough to consume between 50 and 200 pounds of milk daily. And all that nutrient-rich milk goes to good use too, as a newborn blue gains an average of 10 pounds an hour.

Taking Their Time

The magicicada, a winged insect from the cicada family, has a lifespan that, barring sudden death by a predator, is the envy of many other varieties of insects. On average, the magicicada lives 13 to 17 years, and most of that time is spent as a baby or juvenile. These babies bore into the ground, feed off roots and don't see the light of day until somewhere between their 13th and 17th springs. That's when they venture out, make their final transformation into an adult and look forward to their last few weeks of life, at which time they mate, reproduce and die.

Who Am I?

A pig isn't really a pig—it's a hog. The term "pig" technically refers to a baby hog less than 10 weeks old—if indeed the newborn survives that long. Mama pigs under extreme stress have been known to eat their young.

What Are You Called?

Most of us know a baby cow is called a calf, and a baby dog is called a pup, but just what are other babies in the animal world called? Here a few examples:

☞ Young zebras and horses are both called foals.

☞ A baby tortoise is a hatchling.

☞ A baby eel is known as an elver.

☞ A pup refers to a young dog, as well as a baby seal or shark. The confusion comes in when you learn that a young shark is also called a cub or seal.

☞ A cygnet is a baby swan.

☞ Young kangaroos and koalas are both called joeys.

☞ Ever heard the phrase "small fry?" Perhaps it came about because young fish are called fry. Prophetic, don't you think?

☞ A baby frog is known by two names: tadpole and froglet.

☞ A goat baby is a kid, and a ferret baby is a kit.

☞ Young salmon are called parr or smolt.

☞ A baby oyster is nothing but a spat.

☞ A fledgling refers to a young bird whose feathers has just come in and is ready to fly.

☞ Squabs are baby pigeons.

☞ Young rabbits are called leverets.

Survival of the Fittest

Honing a survival instinct is something some sharks learn even before they're born. That's because a tiger shark's eggs are fertilized inside the female's body and, like mammals, the mother gives birth to live babies. This sounds all well and good, but fertilized eggs are not nourished by the mother via the placenta, so there's only one way these babes will make it to birth—by eating any unfertilized embryos and the smaller, weaker pups among them.

Look Out Below!

Giraffes are majestic creatures. Tall and willowy, they can tower a full 19 feet. Of course, anything that big can't help but stumble upon a few limitations in life, and for the females of the species, giving birth is just one of them. Mama can't exactly get comfortable when giving birth, so baby literally falls into the world—about five feet to the ground. In any case, it doesn't seem to hurt the little gaffer. Within a half hour of being born, baby giraffes can stand and can run within 10 hours.

Killing Its Young

Infanticide in the world of rats isn't uncommon, though cases of this usually occur with the youngest newborns. Scientists speculate the reasons for this are numerous and varied. A mother rat may believe some of her young won't survive, so she'll spare them the misery of dying a slow death.

In other cases, the mother might mistake some of her young for a predator. This can happen when someone other than the mother (a human caregiver, for example) washes the newborn before the mother rat has a chance to identify it as her own. Stress can sometimes cause this reaction, as well as the need for a food source, and finally—according to one source—baby rats appear to taste good to other rats. Ewww!

Talk About Extremes

While a full-grown, male kangaroo can reach a height of six and a half feet and weigh in at about 200 pounds, with a birth weight of less than a gram, a baby kangaroo is among the smallest of live births in the mammal world. That's because when it's born, at about 36 days' gestation, the joey isn't fully developed and is actually still the equivalent of the embryonic stage of a human birth. It will take another nine months before the joey is ready to meet the big world outside mama's pouch.

DID YOU KNOW?

Baby dolphins nurse several times an hour, but only for about 10 seconds each time. The amount the baby takes in is enough to have it up and swimming with its mother within an hour of birth. Of course, mama does help a little by creating a current that helps keep baby close to her.

I Vant to Suck Your Blood!

Vampire bats are one of three bat species that feed exclusively off the blood of living animals, and nature has prepared them for this little nutritional oddity with specifically designed fangs. These fangs painlessly cut into the skin of their next meal—in fact, it's so painless that the bat could be feeding for quite a while before its "dinner" knows anything about it. A baby vampire bat's teeth, however, aren't immediately up to that task. At birth, a vampire bat's fangs are hooked. The babies use their teeth to cling to their mothers when flying, and since babies are nursed for 10 months, these rounded teeth make the task a little less uncomfortable for mama!

Tickling the Ivory

The ivory tusks jutting from the lip of an elephant are almost as distinctive as the giant mammal itself. But not all tusks are the same. Newborn elephants are born with milk tusks—tusks that will fall away, like baby teeth do in a human child, and are replaced with permanent tusks. An elephant's teeth, however, are replaced with a new set several times during its lifetime.

Great Expectations

If you thought nine months of pregnancy was tough, just think on these stats for a few moments:

- ☛ Mama rhinos are pregnant for 16 months before giving birth.

- ☛ If you think that's a long time, an elephant—the largest land animal—is pregnant for 22 months.

- ☛ A female whale is usually pregnant for 12 to 14 months, depending on the species.

- ☛ Mama dolphins are pregnant for about one year before baby emerges.

☛ It can take almost two years before some mothers in the shark world give birth to their young. Scientists believe that at about 22 months, the spiny dogfish shark has the longest gestation period.

☛ Aside from the day she gives birth, a female kangaroo is always pregnant. However, she has the ability to stop the development of an embryo until the joey she's just given birth to is ready to leave her pouch.

Turnabout

The seahorse is the only species known in which the male carries and delivers the unborn "fry." Here's the way this works—the female implants her eggs into the male's pouch. The male then carries the eggs until they're ready to be born, which can take anywhere from two to four weeks. When the time is right, he'll birth the babies or expel them from his pouch, with the help of muscular contractions.

Now here's the best part. The male seahorse usually gives birth at night, and by morning, he's ready for the implantation of the next batch. And we think women have it tough!

ABOUT THE AUTHOR

Lisa Wojna

Lisa is the co-author of more than a dozen trivia books, as well as being the sole author of nine other non-fiction books. She has worked in the community newspaper industry as a writer and journalist and has traveled all over the world. Although writing and photography have been a central part of her life for as long as she can remember, it's the people behind every story that are her motivation and give her the most fulfilment.

ABOUT THE ILLUSTRATORS

Peter Tyler

Peter is a graduate of the Vancouver Film School's Visual Art and Design, and Classical animation programs. Though his ultimate passion is in filmmaking, he is also intent on developing his draftsmanship and storytelling, with the aim of using those skills in future filmic misadventures.

Roger Garcia

Roger Garcia is a self-taught artist with some formal training who specializes in cartooning and illustration. He is an immigrant from El Salvador, and during the last few years, his work has been primarily cartoons and editorial illustrations in pen and ink. Recently he has started painting once more. His work can be seen in newspapers, magazines, promo material and on www.rogergarcia.ca

MORE TRIVIA FROM BLUE BIKE BOOKS...

Bride's Book of Traditions, Trivia & Curiosities
by Rachel Conard & Lisa Wojna
There is much tradition and folklore surrounding weddings. Generation after generation, cultures have developed rituals, superstitions and events to make this day a special one to remember. The book covers everything from why women often choose to wear white to the circumstances under which cousins are allowed to marry and so much more wedding trivia from around the world.
$14.95 • ISBN13: 978-1-897278-51-2 • 5.25" x 8.25" • 224 pages

Bathroom Book of Christmas Trivia
by Lisa Wojna
Christmas—a time of peace on Earth and goodwill towards all—is also a time of gift-buying craziness and rampant commercialism. How did we get from the birth of Jesus to department store Santas? Read about the traditions and superstitions surrounding one of our most important holidays and learn how other cultures celebrate the season.
$14.95 • ISBN13: 978-1-897278-26-0 • 5.25" x 8.25" • 224 pages

Dog Trivia
Humorous, Heartwarming & Amazing
by Wendy Pirk
Humans have lived alongside dogs for millennia, but there's more to them than just tail wags, a love for car rides and chasing tennis balls. It is not surprising that there are so many weird facts and fascinating tales about "man's best friend."
$14.95 • ISBN13: 978-1-897278-36-9 • 5.25" x 8.25" • 208 pages

Cat Trivia
Humorous, Heartwarming, Weird & Amazing
by Diana MacLeod
The most popular pet in North America is mysterious yet companionable, ferocious but cuddly, wild and domestic. Cats fascinate us with their exotic yet familiar ways. For cat lovers, this is a must-have.
$14.95 • ISBN13: 978-1-897278-26-0 • 5.25" x 8.25" • 224 pages

Available from your local bookseller or
by contacting the distributor,

Lone Pine Publishing
1-800-518-3541

www.lonepinepublishing.com